The Cri

H. De Vere Stacpoole

Alpha Editions

This edition published in 2022

ISBN : 9789356082526

Design and Setting By
Alpha Editions
www.alphaedis.com
Email – info@alphaedis.com

CHAPTER I

THE ROAD TO NIKKO

"Upon the road to Nikko,Where the pilgrims pray,Along the road to NikkoEither side the way,Thundering great camellia treesDecked with blossoms gay,Adorn the road to Nikko,The mountain road to Nikko,In the month of May."

The singer stopped singing and began to whistle. Then he broke out into prose.

"Damn boots! I'll be lame in another mile. Why can't we be content with sandals like our 'brithers' the Japs!"

"Dinna damn boots, but their makers," replied his companion, a sandy Scot of fifty or more, dressed in broadcloth and a bowler, a figure at once a blot upon the lonely road and a blasphemy against Japan—a blot whose name was M'Gourley. "I vara well remember when I was in Gleska—"

"Oh, don't!" said the poet of the Nikko road, Dick Leslie by name, a young man, or rather a man still young, very tall, straight, dark, and good-looking, and a gentleman from the crown of his close-clipped, curly black head to the soles of the boots that were torturing him. "Don't haul up your factory chimneys, your smoke and whisky bottles in this place of places. I believe if a Scot ever gets into heaven he'll start his first conversation with his first angel by making some reference to Gleska: Look there!"

"Whaur?"

"There!" cried Leslie, turning from the direction of Fubasami and the beginning of the great Nikko valley before them, and pointing backwards away towards Kureise over an expanse of distant country where the clouds were drawing soft shadows across the rice fields and the sinuous hills; over little woods of fir and cryptomeria trees, lakes where the lotus flowers spread in summer, and the king-fisher flashed like a jewel; over occasional fields of flowers, flowers that grew by the million and the million.

Many of these details were absorbed and dulled by distance, yet still lent their spirit to the scene, producing a landscape most strange and quaint.

Nearly every other country seems flung together by nature, but Japan seems to have been imagined by some great artist of the ancient days—imagined and constructed.

"Look there," said Leslie, "saw you ever anything better than that in Clackmannan?"

"Ay, have I," replied M'Gourley, contemplating the view before him, "many's the time. What sort of country do you call that? Man! I'd as soon live on a tea-tray if I had ma choice."

"Well, you've lived in Japan long enough to be used to it. It's always the way; put a man in a paradise like this where there are all sorts of flowers and jolly things around him, and he starts grumbling and growling and pining after rain, and misery, and cold, and sleet, and peat smoke—if he's a Scotchman. How long have you been in Japan, Mac, did you say?"

"Near ever since the Samurai took off their swords and turned policemen."

"What kept you in the East so long if you don't like it?"

"Trade, like the wind, blaweth where it listeth, and a man must e'en follow his trade," said M'Gourley; and they resumed their road.

They were walking to Nikko together, this strangely assorted pair, strangely assorted though they were both Scotchmen. They were approaching the place, not by that splendid avenue of cryptomeria trees that leads from Utso-no-Miya, but by the wild hill road, which runs from Kureise, or rather by the higher hill road, for there are two, and they had taken the loneliest and the longest by mistake (M'Gourley's fault, though he swore that he knew the country like the palm of his hand).

They had come twenty or twenty-five miles of the way by riksha, and were now hoofing the remainder, their luggage having been sent on to Nikko by train.

"And talking of trade," said M'Gourley, "let's go back to the matter we were on a moment ago; there's money in it, and I know the beesiness. I ken it fine; never a man knows better the Jap Rubbish trade."

"You were talking of starting at Nagasaki."

"Ay, Nagasaki's best."

"Well, I'll plank the money," said Leslie. "I'll put up a thousand against a thousand of yours."

M'Gourley stopped and held out a hand sheathed in a mournful-looking black dogskin glove.

"Is't a bargain?" said he.

"It's a bargain. Funny that we should have only met the other day in Tokyo, and that you should have come along to Nikko to show me the sights. I believe all the time you were bent on trepanning me into this business."

"I was that," said M'Gourley, with charming frankness; "for your own good. A man without a beesiness is a man astray, and when you told me in the hotel in Tokyo you were a boddie with money, and nothing to do with it, I said: 'Here's my chance.'"

"If I had met you two months ago," said Leslie bitterly, "I wouldn't have been much use, for my father would not have been dead, and I would not have come into his money. Do you know what I have been?—I have been a remittance man."

"I've met vera much worse people than some of *them*," said Mac, who if his newly found partner had declared himself a demon out of Hades would perhaps have made the same glossatory remark—the capital being assured.

"I'm hanged if I have," said Leslie bitterly. "Give me a Sydney Larrikin, a Dago, a Chinee, before your remittance man. I know what I'm talking about for I have been one—see?"

"What, may I ask—" began M'Gourley, then he paused.

"You mean what was the reason of my being flung off by my father? Youthful indiscretions. Let's sit down; I want to take my boot off."

The road just here took a bend, and became wilder and more lovely, a stream gushed from the bank on which they took their seats, and before them lay a little valley, a valley hedged on either side by cypress trees, and thronged with crimson azaleas.

CHAPTER II

THE BLIND ONE

Crimson azaleas in wild profusion, here struck with sun, here shadowed by the cypress trees—a sight to gladden the heart of a poet. Between the cypress trees, beyond the azaleas, beyond country broken by sunlight and cloud shadows, lay the sea hills of Tanagura in the dimmest bluest distance.

"If I could get that into a gold frame," said Leslie, as he inhaled the delicious perfume of the azaleas and bathed his naked foot in the tiny cascade breaking from the bank on which they sat, "I'd take it to London and send it to the Academy—and they'd reject it."

"Vara likely," replied Mac. "It is no fit for a peecture. Who ever saw the like of yon out of Japan? It's nought but a fakement."

"I say," said Leslie, "talking of fakements—in this business of ours I hope we'll steer clear of all that."

"In this beesiness of oors," said Mac, "I thought you distinctly understood my friend Danjuro will be the nominal head of the firrm—we are but the sleeping pairtners."

Mac's Scotch bubbled in him when he grew excited, or when he forgot himself. Ordinarily he talked pretty ordinary English, but when the stopper was off the Scotch came out, and you could tell by the pronunciation of the word "money" whether he was mentioning the article casually or deep in a deal.

"Well," said Leslie, "I don't want my dreams troubled by visions of Danjuro swindling unfortunate tourists; you say we're to export things, but I don't want to have him roping in people, selling them five-shilling pagodas at five pounds a-piece."

Mac sighed as if with regret at the impossibility of such a delightful deal as that.

"It's rather jolly going into business," continued Leslie, dreamily gazing at the azaleas. "Only crime I've never committed, except murder and a few others. Good God! when I started in life I never thought I'd end my days peddling paper lanterns, and cheating people into buying penny-a-dozen kakemonos for a shilling a-piece. Don't talk to me; all trade is cheating."

"You should have known Macbean," said M'Gourley, who had also taken off his boots and stockings and was bathing his broad splay feet in the pretty little torrent.

"Who was he?"

"Forty year ago I was his 'prentice. Mummies, and idols, and pagods, and scarabeuses was the output of the firm, and Icknield Street, Birmingham, its habitation."

"Idols?"

"Ay, idols. Some the size of your thumb, and some the size of bedposts, which they were derived from; some with teeth, and some with hair, and some bald as a bannock. We stocked half West Africa with idols, and the South Seas absorbed the balance."

"Well, you certainly take the cake," said Leslie.

"I took three pun ten a week at Macbean's, and learnt more eelementary theology than's taught in the schules of Edinboro'. Macbean said artistical idols was what the savages wanted, and what they would get as long as old bedposteses were to be bought at knockdown prices, and sold for the waurth of elephants' tusks."

"You disgust me," said Leslie, "upon my word you do."

"That's what Macbean said one day to the boddie I had in mind when I began telling you of this. The boddie came in grumbling about a mummy—a vara fine mummy it was, too—that had been sold to him for export. The mummy had been stuftit with newspapers, but the *sachrum ustum* used for coloring the stuffing matter being omitted, the printed matter remained in eevidence when the American who bought the article in Cairo opened it to hunt for amulets and scarabeuses. 'Newspapers!' said Macbean. 'And what more do you expect in a fifty-shullin' mummy? Did y' expect it stuffed wi' dimonds?'"

"Well?" said Leslie.

"That's all, and that's the whole of beesiness in a walnut shell; y' canna expect a fifty-shullin' mummy to be stuffed with—"

"Rubbish! the whole of swindling, you mean. Anyhow, we'll keep straight, if you please; a fair profit I don't mind, but I object to rank trickery—by the way, what's the time? my watch has stopped; and how far is Nikko off?"

"It's after two," said Mac, who had no very definite idea of how far Nikko might be off, having led his companion by the wrong road and concealed the fact. "And Nikko is maybe twarree miles, maybe a bit more—wull we go?"

For all answer Leslie took some bar-chocolate from his pocket, gave some to his companion, and proceeded to lunch.

"I daresay you think it funny," said he at last, "my chumming up, and in your heart of hearts—that is, your business heart (excuse me for being frank)—you must think it strange I should put up my money with a man whom I don't know in the least. But, man! the truth of the matter is I'm weary for a friend. I have money enough and to spare, but—I'm weary for a friend.

"I'm the lonest man in the world," went on Leslie, munching his chocolate and gazing at the beautiful scene before him; "the lonest man on God's earth. What is the matter with me that I should never have found and kept a friend? If God had ever given me anything to love I'd have cherished it, but—there is no God that I can see."

"Whisht, man," said Mac. "Dinna talk like that."

"I know I was wild," went on Leslie, "before I left England, but other men have been as bad. I quarreled with my father, but other men's fathers are different from what mine was. He drove me beyond the sea to be an alien and an outcast. I've seen drunken loafers in the bars of Sydney, where I was stuck as a remittance man three years; they had friends of a sort—friends who stuck them, but friend or dog never stuck to me."

"No wumman?" asked M'Gourley, spitting out the remains of the chocolate he was eating, and lighting a vile-looking Hankow cigar.

"I loved a woman once," said Leslie, staring before him with eyes that saw not Japan or the cypress trees or the azaleas. "Her name was Jane Deering; we were boy and girl together, cousins, and her people lived quite close to mine. We got engaged, and were to have been married, and—she threw me over."

"For why?" asked Mac.

"Said she didn't want to get married."

"Well, that was deefinite."

"Damned definite. What's that noise?"

"Tap, tap, tap." It was the tapping of a stick upon the ground, and a man in the dress of a coolie, with a saucer-shaped hat upon his head, turned the corner of the road, coming in the direction of Nikko. He was tapping the ground before him with a staff. He was blind.

"What an awful-looking face!" said Leslie, as the figure approached. "Look, Mac! Did you ever see the like of that?"

One sees many extraordinary and sinister faces in the East, but the face of the on-comer would have been hard to match, even in the stews of Shanghai.

The nose seemed to have been smashed flat by a blow. The face was flat and possessed an awful stolidity, so that at a little distance one could have sworn that it was carved from stone. It impressed one as the countenance of a creature long in communion with evil.

The two Scotchmen held motionless to let this undesirable pass, but he must have possessed some sixth sense, for instead of passing he stopped and begun to whine.

He spoke in a light, flighty, chanting voice, like the voice of a man either insane or delirious.

"What's he say?" asked Leslie.

"He's a Chinee, and wants money."

"Tell the beast to go."

"Says he knows we're foreigners."

"Clever that; why, even I can hear your Scotch sticking out of the gibberish you're talking."

"Says he wants opium—hasn't had any the whole day, and if we will give him opium, or money to buy it, he'll show us things."

"What things?"

"Lord sakes! the creeture's daft; says he can make great magic—snakes out of mud or flowers out of nothing."

"Why doesn't he make some opium if he's so clever?"

"Says the woods around here are full of devils."

"Tell him to show us a devil, then."

Mac translated and the person so well acquainted with devils made answer.

"For a piece of gold he will show us one. Why, Leslie, man, don't you be a fule."

Leslie had taken half a sovereign from his pocket.

"Give it him and tell him to show us a devil, and if he plays any tricks I'll chivy him into Nikko, and give him up to the police."

"Don't be a fule," said Mac testily. "A'weel!"

Leslie put the piece of gold into the creature's hand, who put it to his ear for a moment, and then hid it in his rags. Then he bent his head sideways to the road.

"What's he doing now?"

"He's listening if the road's clear; he says there's nothing on it for two ri on either side, but he hears seven rikshas coming in the direction of Nikko, but he'll have time to do what he wants before they arrive."

The Blind One bent down rapidly and traced an almost perfect circle around himself in the dust of the road; then hurriedly outside this he traced what an initiate might have taken for the form of the Egg, the horns of Simara, and another form needless to describe. Then he said something to Mac.

"He says, we're not to speak, or touch the circle or go near it. I have not paid for this entertainment, and I juist think I'll take a bit walk doon the road."

"Sit down, you old coward," said Leslie. "I'm the one that has paid, and I'm the one the 'deevil' will carry off if there is a deevil. Look!"

The Blind One took from his rags a cane pipe such as blind men use in Japan, only larger, and began to blow mournful notes out of it. It was as strange a sound as ever left human lips, now ear-piercing, now low, low and soothing; his face flushed and swelled; he seemed enraptured, entranced with his own music, and the searching sound of it caused things to move disturbedly in the trees around, and a low croaking, as if from some feathered creature disturbed, to come from the cypress wood.

As he played, he turned north, south, east, and west, lingering, at last, with the reed pipe pointing between the cypress trees, as though he were calling to the blue hills in the distance.

As he stood thus, Leslie, who had been looking at the mysterious symbols around the circle, was seized with an impish impulse, and leaning forward with his walking-stick, he made in the dust inside the circle, and just behind the Blind One's heel, the form of a cross.

In doing this, the point of the stick touched the Blind One's heel.

CHAPTER III

THE LOST ONE

A congreve rocket incautiously touched by a match could not have given a more surprising result.

Flinging the pipe from him with a yell, the Blind One sprang clear over the circle, and stood for an instant panting and blowing at the sun.

He seemed blowing away things that were trying to enter his mouth; then, the staff attached by a thong to his wrist flying about wildly, he began to tear at himself all over his body and fling things away from him, as though he were attacked by a hundred thousand scorpions; then as if bitten by some more serious enemy, he seized his staff, and striking about him wildly, began to run. Hither and thither, hitting right and left, dashing against trees and seeming utterly regardless of them, bleeding, torn, and all the time fighting his phantom pursuers he ran till he vanished round the bend leading towards Nikko. The two Scotchmen ran to the bend of the road, and there down the road they saw him still running, and fighting as if for his life; striking above him as if at things in the air, and around him as if at things leaping at him from the ground. Suddenly he vanished round a further bend, and was lost to view.

"He's gone gyte!" said Mac as they returned.

"Well, I'm damned!" said Leslie.

"I touched his heel, and I suppose he thought it was one of the devils—mad fool!"

"'Tis no madness," said Mac. "If ever I saw a man chased by deevils I've seen one now. 'Twas that mark you made let them loose, or my name's not Tod M'Gourley. Did you no ken you were makin' the sign of the cross in yon damned circle of his? Hech, man! *Look there!*"

"Where?"

"My God!" said M'Gourley, "look you there, *there!* There's a bairn amongst the azaleas!"

"So there is!" said Leslie. "By Jove, a little Jap girl come out of the wood."

"Dom it, man," roared M'Gourley, "she wasn't there twarree seconds ago. She's come out of no wood; she's been *fetched.*"

"Well, of all the superstitious idiots!" said Leslie, gazing from the perspiring M'Gourley to the figure of the quaint and pretty little Japanese girl who was busy amidst the azaleas plucking the blossoms. "Why, it wouldn't take her more than 'twarree seconds' to come out of the wood. Anyhow, I'll go and see if she's real."

"Man! man! hauld back!" cried the agonized M'Gourley as his partner plunged amidst the bushes. "Ye'll be had; she's a bogle. Lord's sake! Lord's sake! Well, gang your own gate, I'm off to Nikko."

Yet he waited.

The bogle was plucking blossoms as hard as she could and in the profuse manner of childhood. She and the azaleas made a sight for sore eyes.

She might have been seven or eight, dressed in a blue kimono with a scarlet obi, hair black as ebony shavings, tightly drawn off the forehead and held up with a tortoiseshell comb—the "germ of a woman."

Her back was turned to Leslie, and as he got within arm's length of the quaint and delicious little figure he did just what you or I might have done—bent down, seized her up, and kissed her.

The bogle dropped her flowers and gave a shriek, a most distinctly human shriek.

"He's kessed her!" cried M'Gourley, addressing the azaleas, the cypress trees, and all Japan.

Then he stood in agony, held to the spot by the sight of Leslie and the bogle making friends.

It didn't seem to take long, for presently he returned through the azaleas triumphant, carrying her in his arms.

"Here's your bogle," said he, placing her on the dusty road where, with all the gravity of the Japanese child, she made a deep obeisance to M'Gourley. That gentleman returned the compliment with a short, sharp nod.

"I'm awa' to Nikko," said he in the hard, irritable voice of a person who is desirous of avoiding an undesirable acquaintance, gazing at Leslie and steadily ignoring the lady in blue who was now holding on to Leslie's right leg, contemplating M'Gourley, and sucking the tip of a taper and tiny forefinger all at the same time. "I'm awa' to Nikko. 'Tis no place for a mon like me. Never was I used to the company of fules—"

"Don't be an ass! Speak to her; you have the tongue, and I haven't."

"I winna."

"Well, of all the old women I ever met," said Leslie, addressing a "thundering great camellia tree" that stood opposite, "this partner of mine takes the bun!—don't he, Popsums?" bending down and looking into the small face, the left cheek of which was now resting against his knee.

Popsums, in reply to the smile and interrogative tone in the question she did not understand, smiled gravely back and murmured something that sounded like "Hei."

M'Gourley snorted, and Leslie broke out laughing; he had little of the Japanese, but he knew that "Hei" meant "Yes."

CHAPTER IV

AMIDST THE HILLS

Just then a ripple of laughter came down the breeze, and round the corner of the road, heading for Nikko, came at full trot seven rikshas streaming out like a scarf of color; a dream of color—for each riksha contained a lady most beautiful to behold under the splendor of her umbrella.

They were a party of girls returning to Nikko after some sylvan freak, and they drew up as if by common assent to admire the azaleas.

Leslie, removing his hat and lifting his treasure trove, held her up for exhibition.

The girls laughed and spoke to her; had they been English girls she would have been promptly handed round and kissed; and she, with becoming gravity, replied gracefully in a few half-lisped words.

Then, leaving behind them on the air a cloud of dust, a perfume of camellia oil, and a long drawn "Sayonara," the bevy of beauties passed in a gorgeous flight of mixed colors round the bend of the road and were gone.

"Ye mind he said seven rikshas were coming," cried Mac.

"Bother!" answered Leslie. "He'd come the same direction and passed them. Do you think they'd have laughed and spoken to her if there was anything wrong and they're Japs, and ought to know. Come! buck up, man! You're not afraid to do what a girl has done?"

"A'weel!" said M'Gourley, half ashamed of himself; and dour as any Procurator Fiscal, he set to the examination of the being who was now on the ground again, her hand clasped in that of Leslie.

This was the result of the examination. Deponent lived with her father. Where? She did not know.—Just beyond there somewhere. What was the house like she lived in? It had a plum-tree growing before it. What did her father do? He hammered things with a hammer. Had she any brothers and sisters? No; but—sudden thought—she had a sugar-candy dragon, and she had lost it. (Here deponent wept slightly and with reserve.)

Pause in the interrogations whilst a snub nose was wiped with Leslie's pocket handkerchief.

And a kite, but that was at home. She had gone that day with a little boy—a neighbor—to hunt for the saccharine dragon, and they had lost themselves, then they had lost each other, then *she* had lost herself. How was that possible? Well, she had gone to sleep. Where? In the wood.

Here the examinate went off into a tale about an impossible tom-cat with wings, which she had once seen on an umbrella, and beheld once again in the wood, but was suppressed by the court and asked to keep to facts.

Whilst asleep in the wood she was awakened, so she declared, by a sound like the passage of a flight of storks, and, coming out of the wood, fearful of meeting a dragon, she began to pick the pretty flowers; then she was seized by the honorable gentleman, whose height was greater than a poplar tree.

How old was she? Eight times the cherry blossom had blown since her humble self had come into the world.

Then she volunteered the entirely unsolicited statement that it was likely her little boy companion had been lost in the snow. But that was impossible— well, it was a field of lilies then—and he had been most possibly devoured by a dragon.

What did she propose about going home? Did she know the way, and could she go alone?

Here she declared herself utterly at a loss. Her home was somewhere near by, but where, she could not exactly say.

"Well, well!" said M'Gourley, when he had finished his examination. "It seems to me that bogle or no bogle you've saddled yoursel' wi' a lost child. Whaur's your common sense now?"

"Just where it always was.—Question is—what are we to do? Can *you* suggest anything?"

"Na, na! it's not for me to say," said the other, with that vile sense of satisfaction a brither Scot feels when a brither Scot has made a cubby of himself. Then, remembering the bond of partnership, "If I were the party responsible, I'd just pop her back where I fund her first, and rin."

"Well, you *are* a beast! Why, you benighted old mummy-stuffer, I believe you've got a scarab in your bosom instead of a heart! I'll take her along to Nikko, and get the police to hunt out her home. Stay, we haven't asked her what's her name."

M'Gourley asked the question, and the Lost One declared her name to be "Bell-flower."

"Bell-flower!" said Leslie, who had a smattering of botany, "that's a campanula. We'll call her—'Campanula.'"

She also made declaration that she was quite satisfied to go with the honorable gentleman, whose height exceeded the tallest of trees. Leslie lifted her up and seated her upon his shoulder, and, as they started, he turned and looked back at the loveliness of the perfumed azalea valley—a sight that was yet to haunt him in the time to come.

"It's my opeenion," said M'Gourley, as they took the road, "that there was something forming in yon wood, something dom bad, and you flung it out of the forming eelement, and she was just suckid in."

"What d'you mean?"

"The wraith of some dead bairn was wanderin' aboot, and the forming eelement seized it."

"What forming element? Rubbish! That chap was a lunatic; well, when he felt me touch him it set his lunacy off, that's all. Why, I once went to a big asylum in Scotland, and I saw a man cutting just the same capers, fighting devils. He's an opium taker, and the opium is out of his brain, that's all. Drink does the same thing—Hi! By Jove, look up there! He's at it still."

Away up in the wild mountain gorge they saw a figure. It was the Blind One still pursued, still running, and apparently fighting for his life. If his actions were not the outcome of insanity they gave food to the mind for the most terrible suppositions.

Streaming with blood from his mad dashes against the trees, he seemed surrounded on all sides, hemmed in, fighting furiously like a man surrounded by wolves. If a tree chanced to be near, an opening seemed to be made for him by his tormentors towards it, and he would rush at it and dash himself against it, falling back bleeding but fighting still, screaming and all the time being steadily shepherded further and further into the loneliness of the hills.

"Sirs! Sirs!" cried Mac, throwing up his hands as the horrible spectacle vanished round a distant bend of the gorge. "This is no sight for a Christian mon!"

"It's pretty rotten," said Leslie who looked rather pale and sick. "Fetch out that flask of yours, Mac. Thanks. Poor devil! would there be any use following him?"

"Not for twanty thousand pounds would I follow him," said Mac, gurgling at the flask. "He's in ither hands than ours."

And, indeed, not for a very great sum would Leslie have gone up that desolate gorge to see the finish of the tragedy.

"Let's go on," said Leslie, "and don't let's speak of it again. I want to forget it—ugh!"

CHAPTER V

THE TEA HOUSE OF THE TORTOISE

It was at the next turn that Nikko broke upon them, a long way off, lying in its valley amidst the high hills, hills fledged with greenery to their summit.

There are sights that strike the eye and the heart at the same time, and the sight of Nikko where the Shoguns sleep, Nikko the beautiful in the silent valley, amidst the silent hills, is one of these.

The delicate colors, the exquisite tracery of the temple roofs, the crystal clearness of the air through which the eye can pick out detail after detail, the atmosphere of tranquillity of the mountains, and the green cryptomeria trees, make up a picture, leaving little for the heart to desire, or the imagination to conceive.

"Why," cried Leslie, turning to his companion (Campanula was seated aloft in solitary state upon his shoulder clutching his hair tight, whilst he held in one big hand her two little sandal-shod, tabi-clad feet), "if that's Nikko, it's ten miles off if it's a foot. What've you got to say for yourself, hey?"

"A'weel," said M'Gourley, glowering at Nikko, "if you want my candid opeenion, we've juist gone astray; the country I know well, but these dom roads lead one like a Jack o'Lanthorn. It's my opeenion that a Japanese road—"

"I don't want your opinion on Japanese roads, I want your concise opinion about yourself—ain't you a fool?"

"Ay, ay," said M'Gourley, as if considering the matter, "a fule I may be, but it's my candit opeenion that I'm not the only fule in Japan."

"Well," said Leslie, "fool or no fool, we'll have to tramp it, and you'll have to take your turn to carry the kid, so—*Marchons!*"

Campanula, so far from being frightened at her awful elevation from the earth, seemed to enjoy the situation, and to find food for a sort of muse of her own, for she began to hum as Leslie took the road with his long stride, and to sing in a lisping sort of way.

"What's she singing?" demanded her bearer of the sweating Scot at his side.

"Lord knows! 'tis an eldritch chune, and I dinna like to listen to the words. Man, Leslie, but your legs are longer than mine, and I canna keep the pace."

"Well, I'll go slower if you'll listen, and tell me what she's singing."

"She's singing," gasped M'Gourley, "s' far as I can make out, some diddering noensense aboot a sugar-candy dragon that a man like a poplar tree is goin' to hunt, he and a man like a corbie."

"That's you."

"More like some bogle from the wood that's maybe after us now. I am not a supersteetious man—na, na! ye may laugh or not—but would y' like to know what in my humble opeenion you are cartin' on your shoulders?"

"Yes?"

"Some bairn that has been lost and dead these years, and has been whustled up by that blind deevil with the pipe. What did she mean by that reeference to the snaw—answer me that!"

"When I can get into the mind of a Japanese child, and see the world as it sees it, I'll answer you; you know what children's minds are, how they mix and imagine things."

"What did she mean by that reeference to the snaw?" grimly went on M'Gourley. "Mix or no mix, what did she mean by the other bairn being lost in the snaw?"

"Well," said Leslie, "I don't care a button whether she's a bogle or not. If she is, she's the prettiest bogle that was ever bogled, and about the heaviest, I should think. Here, you take a turn with her, I'm about done."

They took it turn about, M'Gourley vastly loth, to carry the Lost One; and the Lost One stopped them to gather flowers for her by the wayside, to give her drinks from rivulets, to help her admire and wonder at herons and other marvels of the way, so that it was after six of the clock when two of the most dusty and perspiring Scotchmen in the Eastern Hemisphere entered the happy village of Nikko from the mountain side, Campanula this time on Leslie's shoulder, grave, triumphant, and holding a huge lily in her hand.

Nikko and its surroundings just now was ablaze with scarlet japonica. The lamps of the camellias were lit, the soaring wistaria vines had broken into clusters of pale lilac blossoms, the iris beautified the field, and the wild cherry the thicket. It was as if spring had called from the tomb of Iyeyasu and her faithful had come to pray.

There are two hotels at Nikko known to the globe-trotter, "Kanayas" and the "New Nikko," but M'Gourley knew a better place than these.

As they passed down the long inclined street a baby with a shaved head, a baby that was half a baby and half an obi, tied behind in a stiff and preposterous bow, spied Campanula being borne aloft, dropped his immediate business—the attempt to fly a kite shaped like a moth—and followed the newcomers with a shout.

The shout, as if by magic, brought half a dozen children from nowhere in particular; girl children with dolls on their backs, older girl children with babies on their backs, boys battledore in hand, and all with clogs on their feet, clogs that went clipper-clapper, waking up the echoes and calling forth more children, so that when they had got half-way down the mile-long street from the upper village Campanula had a "following," the like of which had never been seen, perhaps, since the pied piper passed through Hamelin.

A colored, laughing, murmuring, rippling throng following with every eye fixed on the Lost One borne sky-high on the shoulder of the tall stranger; a throng, the half of which could have walked under a dinner-table without much inconvenience; some empty-handed, some still grasping their implements of play, all agog, yet of decent and orderly behavior. A throng, in fact, of ladies and gentlemen in the making.

Backward over the summit of Leslie gazed Campanula upon this crowd, whilst the stall-keepers and the stray riksha men, the pilgrims and the paupers, the priest and the policeman, stood by the way to watch the procession pass.

"I say," called Leslie to his companion, who was limping behind dead beat, yet in an agony at the "splurge" they were making, "this is gay, isn't it?"

"Dod rot the child!" cried M'Gourley, nearly tumbling over a fat baby with a tufted head, who was running in front of him and trying to look up in his face.

"I dinna ken whoat ye mean by gay. I have no immeediate particular use for the waurd. Never before have I been held up to public reedicule. I'm a decent livin' man, ye ken, an' I ha'na any use for such gayeties. I leave them to ithers who care for makin' assinine eediots of theirselves; but, thank the Laird, we're nearly there noo."

They turned a corner and entered a gate that led to a garden.

At the gate M'Gourley turned and addressed the camp followers, telling them with forced politeness that there was nothing more to be seen; that the show was over, in fact, and asking them honorably to excuse him the pleasure of being followed any more.

The crowd murmured, and dissolved, the earth seemed to take it up like blotting-paper, and M'Gourley, turning his back upon its remnants, led the way through the garden, past a tiny lake in the midst of which stood an island, inhabited by a huge frog, and so, by a path, to the front of a long, low, white-washed house.

This was the Tea House of the Tortoise, a place well known to M'Gourley, as (to use his own abominable expression) being "cheap and clean."

A panel of the front was drawn back, revealing cream-white matting and lamp light.

M'Gourley sat down with a sigh on the side of the veranda, and began to pull off his elastic side boots. Leslie sat down also, with Campanula in his lap; he could not put her down for she had literally tumbled into sleep.

"Pull off my boots, Mac," said he. "I can't let go of this blessed child."

"Na!" said Mac mysteriously, and somewhat viciously, as he knelt down and unlaced his partner's boots, "ye cannot let her go, ye cannot let her go; forby, she wullna let *you* go."

"You think she's going to stick to me?"

"Imphim," replied Mac.

Imphim is not Japanese, it is the double Scotch grunt, which has twenty-two separate meanings, mostly unpleasant. Shut your mouth tight and try to say "Hum, hum," and you will achieve "Imphim," but never do it again, please.

Leslie was about to answer, when a sound behind made him turn, and there, like a pinned-down butterfly, was a Mousmè on the mat, crying, "Irashi, condescend to enter."

M'Gourley—a most unengaging figure in his stocking feet—rose and addressed the Mousmè.

He told her things in language unknown to Leslie; things about the sleeping Campanula evidently, for he pump-handled with his arm in the direction where Leslie, bootless now, sat holding her.

The Mousmè on her knees, a camellia blossom in her hair and her eyes fixed upon M'Gourley, seemed fascinated. Then she called out and....

"Hai tadaima," came a soft voice from somewhere in the back premises, and a second Mousmè appeared, made obeisance, and listened whilst the tale, whatever it was, was laid before her.

Deep astonishment, exclamations of wonder, a call:

"Hai tadaima!" and an old lady appeared, and made obeisance, and listened whilst the thrice-told tale was told her by the two Mousmès and M'Gourley all together.

Meanwhile Leslie, feeling ridiculously like a nursemaid, sat holding the Lost One, whose soul was wandering in the vain land of dreams.

"What are you stuffing those creatures up with?" he suddenly broke out. "Blessed if you oughtn't to be dressed in a kimono and a petticoat; you're the biggest old woman of the lot. Ask one of them to take the kid, or I'll go off to the hotel with her."

"One minit," said Mac. "They're conseedrin' the matter."

Scarce had he spoken when the old lady called out, and entered on the scene, an old gentleman, the proprietor of the tea house, a black cat, and two more Mousmès.

"Oh, *do* call a few more!" said Leslie. "And call in a couple of musicians and make the comic opera complete."

"There are no more to call," replied Mac. "They are conseedrin' the matter. The Japanese are a very supersteetious people, and these are good friends of mine, and I would not spring a pairson upon them with dootful anticeedents. You see, Leslie, man, the presence of the bairn must be explained. She is not a bale of goods we can dump in a corner. Bide a wee; I will talk them over yut."

The Areopagus was considering the question as to whether Campanula, if admitted to the Tea House of the Tortoise, would bring ruin and destruction or a blessing on the premises, when Hedgehog San, the black cat, settled the matter by coming up to Leslie and rubbing against his leg.

Then the Hon. Hedgehog—may his ashes rest in peace!—jumped on Leslie's knee and rubbed himself against Campanula.

That clinched the business.

The old lady herself advanced, and, taking the Lost One from the Weary One, carried her bodily into the house, whilst Leslie, yawning and stretching himself, followed.

Inside, in the bare, clean room, the little Mousmè with the camellia in her hair addressed herself to Leslie in a soft and beseeching voice.

"What does she want?" he asked of Mac.

"She wants to know if you require anything."

"A bath—that's what I want more than anything—don't you?"

"I am not given to promeescuous bathing," said M'Gourley, "being greatly subject to the siatickee; but a bath you wull have, and I'll e'en sit here and smoke a pipe whilst you bathe yourself."

"I want also a sugar-candy dragon for the bairn," said Leslie. "Ask 'em to send out and get one. I suppose you can get such things?"

M'Gourley gave the message to the maid, and she departed.

The travelers' luggage—a frightful-looking old mid-Victorian carpet bag belonging to M'Gourley, and a Gladstone of Leslie's—had already arrived at the tea house, having been sent on by rail *via* Utsu-no-Miya, and the two sat down on small square cushions, placed on the cream-colored matting, to smoke a pipe, whilst dinner and the bath were preparing.

"The police will be here the morn about that bairn," said Mac in his cheerful way, "and we'll have to acoont for her."

"Of course we will."

"Ay, ay," said Mac, "but have you ever acoonted for a thing to the Japanese police?"

"Well, considering I've only been in Japan ten days, I haven't had much time, you see, to fall foul of the police."

"I found a scairf pin once," said this comforter of Job, "on the Bund at Nagasaki. Twa-and-sax-pence it was worth, or maybe three shullin', and I took it to the police office and began to acoont for it."

He stopped and sighed and sucked his pipe.

"Well?"

"Well, I'm acoontin' for it still, and that's three months ago; letters and papers, and papers and letters enough to drive a man daft! Well, I'm thinkin' if a twa-and-saxpenny scairf pin can cause such a wully waugh, what's a live bairn going to do? Now, I'm thinking—"

"May I give you a piece of advice, Mac?"

"I am always open to judeecious advice," answered the unsuspecting Mac.

"Well, don't think too much or you'll hurt yourself."

M'Gourley grunted, and at that moment the Mousmè with the camellia in her hair entered with the announcement that the bath was ready in the room above, and Leslie departed.

"When you have shown the honorable gentleman the bath, come down; I wish to speak to you," said M'Gourley to the lady of the camellia. She obeyed the request and M'Gourley held her in light conversation, till he knew by the sounds above that his partner was in the tub. Then he released the handmaiden, and she departed upstairs.

He listened, and presently he heard Leslie's voice.

"Go away, please. Good heavens I say, I *wish* you'd go away! No, I don't want soap. I say, Mac! Hi, McGourley!—leave my back alone—*M'Gourley*!"

But M'Gourley, like an Indian Sachem, smoked on and answered not.

He was having his revenge for the Nikko road.

CHAPTER VI

THE DREAMER AND THE DRAGON

They had finished dinner; a dinner which began with tea and bean flour cakes, passed on to fish served on little mats of grass, went on to soup served in lacquered bowls, proceeded to prawns; halted, hesitated, and went back to soup, scratched its head, so to speak, and then, as if with an after-thought, served up a quail, apologized for the substantiality of the quail by presenting a salted plum on a little plate, and then harked shamelessly back to soup, ending deliriously with a shower of little dishes containing everything inconceivable, and a big bowl of rice.

This is an impressionist picture of a Japanese dinner. I have eaten many, but I have never carried away more than an impression, and whether kuchi-tori comes before hachiz-a-kana, I cannot say, or where the seaweed or salted fish come in—but come in they do, they and other things stranger than themselves.

A *chamècen* was thrumming somewhere in the house as they dined, sitting on the soft white matting, and waited upon by two Mousmès crouched on the matting like little panthers preparing to spring.

A slid back panel of the front wall made a doorway through which they could see the moon wandering over Nikko, casting her cool white light upon the blazing japonica flowers, the glory of the camellias, the roofs of the temples, and the sad dark beauty of the cryptomeria trees.

Nikko by day is fair, but by night, when the moon is overhead, when the air is full of the sounds of wandering waters, and the wind is heavy with the perfume of the wild azaleas, Nikko is a dream.

When the tea and bean cakes had been served, the moon was in the act of washing weakly a house gable across the garden, and a pale lilac-colored flower of the wistaria, which projected above the extemporized doorway; but by the time the quail had made its appearance, the garden was solid in moonlight, the pond was a mirror, and the frog self-marooned on the little island, was as distinct as if seen by daylight.

"I must learn Japanese," said Leslie, taking a cigarette-case from his pocket and lighting a cigarette at the tobacco-mono that stood at his elbow. "My lines are cast in Japan, that's clear, but a man without the language is a helpless baby."

"Ay, ay," said M'Gourley. "You can easily get instruction in the Japanese: take a wumman to live with you."

"I haven't looked at a woman for ten years, and I don't want to look at one again." Then suddenly bursting out: "Why, you old scamp, talking like that—you told me you were a member of the Free Kirk."

"The Wee Kirk," corrected Mac, leisurely lighting his pipe with an ember from the hibachi.

"Well, Free Kirk or Wee Kirk, you ought to be jolly well ashamed of yourself; and were you a member of the Wee Kirk when you were constructing idols in Birmingham with old What's-his-name?"

"Na, na; those were my godless days. I got my releegion late in life, and a vara good releegion it is; a waurkable releegion, one that does not heat in the bearings, but runs smooth."

"And what is this wonderful religion, if I may ask?"

"It is noet so much wonderful as waurkable, and it may be compreezed in the sentence: 'Do unto ithers as ithers would do unto you.'"

"O good Lord! and you call that a religion! Why, you precious old humbug, that means you can rob, and plunder, and murder, and cheat—that is to say, you can act like a beast towards people who would act so to you."

"Just so."

"Well, there's one thing I like about you, you're frank, to say the least of it."

This remark seemed greatly to incense Mac, who, perhaps, misunderstood the meaning of the word frank.

"When y've been in the waurld as long as I have, surrounded on ivry side by scoondrels and robbers, y'll maybee be as fraunk as mysel'. Fraunk.—wid ye give me a defineetion of the waurd—fraunk! I wid have ye to understand I'm an hoenest mon with hoenest men, but *I'm a scoondrel wi' scoondrels*. Fraunk!" And so he went on, his Scotch accent deepening as deepened his excitement, till at last he broke down into Gaelic, and thundered his remarks at the hibachi, slapping his thigh as he did so, and wakening the echoes of the house, which was resonant as a fiddle. So that by the time he had got to the end of his exordium, Leslie saw a panel waver back an inch, and the lady of the camellia peeping in to see what the Learned One was shouting about.

"Keep your hair on," said Leslie, when Mac, with a final "Fraunk!" delivered in English, began to refill and light his pipe. "I didn't mean to insult you; I only meant to say I like your open-heartedness."

"Ay, I was ever that to those I had a liking for."

"I meant more precisely your open-mindedness—but no matter, let's talk of something else. I wonder where they've put the kid, and oh, by Jove! I wonder if they've got that dragon. Sing out and ask, like a good chap."

Mac clapped his hands, and "Hai tadaima!" came as a response.

It was worth the trouble of clapping one's hands to hear that sweet reply.

A moment later, a panel slid back and the camellia lady appeared.

Campanula San was asleep, and at that very moment Wild-cherry-bud was in search of the Hon. Dragon, with orders to leave no confectioner's stall unvisited till she had secured him.

This with immovable gravity and deep, sweet earnestness of tone.

"Well," said Leslie when she had withdrawn, "of all the people I have struck yet, give me the Japanese."

"Wait till you've had beesiness transactions with them," said Mac darkly. "I am no so unfreenly to the Japs in or'nary life, but in beesiness the Jap's a wrugglin' sairpent—all but one—Danjuro—the man we're going to join in partnership; he's as straight as a Chinee."

"He must be damn crooked then!"

"Cruik'd enough to make his way in Japan, but straight enough to a freend; but you're a poet, man, Leslie, and no beesiness man. I kent y' for a poet when you sang that bit song on the road—the song aboot the camellia trees."

Leslie laughed.

"That rubbish! It's not mine; I read it in the Sydney *Bulletin*. Funny enough, too, it was the first thing that made me think of coming to Japan! Poetry! Good God! Put a man through the remittance mill in Sydney and see all the poetry that will be left in him! Put a butterfly through a sausage machine and then see how beautifully it will fly! Yes, I was once a poet; years and years ago I was a poet—a poet who never wrote anything, but a poet for all that. I could see the beauty of the world; and then they blinded me. Who? I don't know—the world. Maybe it was myself, maybe not. Maybe it was my father, maybe not. I only state the fact that something in me is dead—the something that took joy in life and found beauty in innocence—or was dead till I came to Japan. Oh, M'Gourley, man, the years I've spent in Sydney under a cloud, mixing with bar loafers, cursing my father and myself; the years I've spent in Sydney have broken my soul in me!"

"Why did ye not waurk?"

"Work! I had just enough money to keep me from starvation and decently dressed. I might have got a clerkship; for what good? To make another hundred a year. To spend on what? Can you not understand, man, that my mainspring was gone, that I was put out of the world I knew, tied by the leg to Sydney, bound to appear every quarter-day at the double-damned lawyer's office, or starve? Two things only kept me alive—tobacco and books—saved me from myself and from drink."

"What sort of a mon was your faither?"

"A hard, dour, just man—a man who could make no allowance for folly."

"Ay, ay! Had y' any brithers and sisters?"

"Never a one, and my mother died when I was two; and he used to leather me. Well, you can fancy my joy when old Bloomfield, the lawyer, sent for me one day and said: 'I've bad news for you, Mr. Leslie.' 'What's that?' said I. 'Your father is dead. He died intestate, and you have inherited his property. I am advised it amounts to over twenty-one thousand pounds.'"

"Twenty-one thousand?" said Mac in admiration.

"Yes; and I said to Bloomfield: 'You must be either a fool or a hypocrite, for that's the best news I ever heard in my life, and you know it.' Then some instinct took me over here to Japan. I was thinking of going to England, but I found all at once I had a horror of England and the English, so I came to Japan; and glad I am I came. Can you fancy what these people here are to me after the population of Sydney—those raucous, horse-racing, drink-swilling beasts? Then I fell in with you at Tokyo, and took a fancy to your old Scotch mug—and here we are."

At this moment a little figure crossed the garden, bearing a lantern on the end of a stick. It was Wild-cherry-bud; and presently she appeared with the much-sought-for dragon wrapped in rice paper.

It was a wonderful creation with a twisted tail, rather stumpy wings, but with a mouth that made up for all defects; nothing so ferocious had ever perhaps before been done in sugar candy.

When the thing had been inspected and approved, Wild-cherry-bud led the way to where Campanula slept, for Leslie wished his present to be placed beside her, so that she might find it when she awoke.

The Lost One, looking very much lost indeed on a huge futon (a quilt thicker than a muffin), and covered by a blue mosquito-net with red bound edges, was so profoundly asleep that the clicking of the net being pulled aside and the light of the night lantern borne by Wild-cherry-bud did not disturb her. She was sleeping on her back, the top futon only drawn to her waist, and her little perfectly shaped white hands were crossed pathetically on her breast.

Leslie knelt down, and lifting one little hand placed the long-sought monster beneath it. The hand clasped the dragon, the long-sought dragon, and across the sleeper's face passed what seemed the ghost of a smile.

"A'weel!" thought Mac as he looked on, "had he a bairn he'd make a better faither to it than his own faither made to him."

Then the mosquito-net was drawn and they departed, leaving Campanula to the possession of her dreams.

Up in their room Leslie steadily refused to undress till the waiting Mousmè had "cleared out." He had already refused to allow her to rub his back when he was in his tub and now this—

The Tea House of the Tortoise people, good old-fashioned, Japanese inn people, unused to foreign follies, could not make it out.

The Areopagus convened itself again, and held council by the light of an andon, or night lantern.

"What could it mean?" There was simply no meaning in it. Such a thing had never happened before, and the general conclusion was that Leslie had "gone gyte."

Then the Areopagus went to bed all together under the same mosquito-net, and silence reigned with the moon over the Tea House of the Tortoise. The moon wandering over Nikko touching temple and tea-house pointed a pallid finger between the window chinks of the room where the Lost One lay asleep, as if to show her to the night. Clasping the candy dragon whose ferocious eyes shone carbuncle-like in the placid moonlight she made a strange picture, veiled by the blue gauze of the mosquito-net.

CHAPTER VII

HOW CAMPANULA BROUGHT FORTUNE TO THE HOUSE OF THE TORTOISE—AND OTHER THINGS

The sun rose up and struck Nikko; struck the sacred red lacquered bridge that crosses the foaming river, and the common bridge that you and I may use, the potter's shop, and the golden shrine of Iyeyasu.

Then temple after temple broke up from shadow as the sun reached for them and found them, and the hills took on a momentary splendor, an ethereal loveliness, evanescent as youth and never to be recaptured by the day.

In the garden of the Tea House of the Tortoise a bomb-shell full of bickering sparrows seemed suddenly to burst above the pond, the sun looked over the wall upon the dwarf maples in their blue porcelain flowerpots, a panel of the white house front slid back and a Mousmè appeared, her head tied up in a blue cotton duster; appeared another Mousmè, dragging a futon to air in the morning brightness, and yet another who came out and yawned at the sun, showing him the full extent of her pink gullet, and every one of her thirty-two white teeth.

Then Hedgehog San, a cat honored and beloved, came forth with tail erect, and a grasshopper hanging by the veranda in a tiny cage creaked forth a thin hymn of praise.

Thus started the day at the Tea House of the Tortoise.

When Leslie and M'Gourley came downstairs—a stair like a ship's companion-way but without any balustrade—they found Campanula having her obi tied by Fir-branch (she who had yawned at the sun), and Leslie was informed through his partner that the dragon had been found and that he had grown; this statement, with some confidential information concerning a thunder-cat of which she had dreamed, Mac translated from the original with a serious face.

Up to this he had treated the Lost One as an adult, and as a most undesirable adult, with whom he wished to have nothing to do. But Campanula, fresh and spruce in the light of morning, chattering over her shoulder to you about thunder-cats, whilst Fir-branch tied her obi in a huge bow, was a person whose charm was not to be denied, and Mac began to thaw.

"What's a thunder-cat?" asked Leslie.

"Lord only knows! some contraption in the shape of an animal that makes thunder. The Japs are full of supersteetions about animals. Wull we out before breakfast?"

Leslie the night before had declared his intention of sending for the police next morning before the police sent for him, and had given a message to the landlord accordingly. But he might have saved his breath.

Nikko was agog. Whether the tale had leaked through the chinks of the Tea House of the Tortoise, whether Wild-cherry-bud had distributed it during her peregrinations in search of the dragon, no one will ever know; the fact remains that the story of Campanula had gone abroad with additions—all sorts of weird and wonderful additions. Half Nikko had seen her borne aloft on the shoulders of Leslie, the other half had heard extraordinary statements concerning her origin; the result was that the whole of Nikko ached inwardly with a great ache of curiosity.

By seven o'clock fifteen Mousmès or maybe twenty, had arrived singly and in couples, not to ask questions, but to borrow things, or to offer the loan of things, or to ask after the health of old mother Ranunculus, the landlady of the "Tortoise." Incidentally they learned about Campanula.

A juggler had made her on the Nikko road. Out of what, for goodness' sake? Out of a wild azalea bush!

No!

Yes, assuredly, the Learned One had said so.

And what had become of the juggler? He had vanished in a clap of thunder—turned into a dragon.

Surprising!

And they went off to spread the news.

At half-past eight, or thereabouts, a little man in white, the chief of the Nikko police, arrived. He had come officially, but he also was aching to get to the truth of this marvelous tale.

Now the Japanese police is the most perfect police force in the world in every respect. They are recruited from the Samurai or fighting-class, and they are gentlemen to a man.

The chief of the Nikko police made profound apologies for disturbing the peace of the strangers, then he heard the story told by M'Gourley.

He agreed that it was strange, but opined that the Lost One might simply be a lost child. Where exactly was she found? In a valley of crimson azaleas on the road from Kureise. Ah, yes! there was such a valley well known, for the azaleas were crimson, and differed from the wild scarlet azaleas so common hereabouts. There were also villages around there, and tea houses; it might possibly be that she belonged to one of these. As to the mad man they had seen running away, no one else had seen him.

Then Campanula was brought in and questioned, the whole of the "Tortoise" people squatting round in a ring, even down to Hedgehog San, who sat with judicial gravity, and seemed to be taking mental notes.

She told her little tale about the house with the plum tree in front of it, and the kite, and the sugar-candy dragon which she had lost and found again. How the said dragon had grown very much, and seemed different, but tasted all right. Here she hastened to explain that she had not eaten him, only touched him with her tongue.

She could not possibly say what men called her father. He hammered things. What sort of things? She did not know, but they went pong, pong, pong, when he struck them.

"Tinsmith," murmured M'Gourley.

She was sure of one thing, that her father's house was quite close to the wood and the azalea valley.

How old was she?

Seven times had the cherry blossoms blown since her humble self—

"Hauld there," said M'Gourley. Then in Japanese he explained that yesterday she had declared that eight times the cherry blossoms had blown since her humble self, etc.

Ah, yes! but how was she to know? a lump of mud like her!

In conclusion, she took back her statement about the snow. She must have dreamt that in the wood.

Then the court began to consult, the "lump of mud" sitting in their midst pensive and rather sad, a scarlet flower in her black hair, and the bow of her obi looking very stiff and huge.

"Look here," said Leslie at last. "Tell him I'll look after her, and pay all expenses till she's found. Tell him to have the place searched, all that wood and country, and I'll pay for it; and if they can't find her people I'll adopt her. I will, begad!"

Mac translated.

At first the chief of police seemed to think that the "lump of mud" should be hauled off to the police office—impounded, in short; then M'Gourley intervened. M'Gourley was a power in Japan just then, for the astute Scot had made himself very useful to the government in past years, and the chief of police, when he heard what Mac had to say, agreed to leave matters where they were whilst the country was being searched, and the chief of police at Tokyo communicated with.

Then he took his departure, and here began the prosperity of the Tea House of the Tortoise.

Three elderly gentlemen in kimonos were the first to arrive; after them a youth in a bowler hat, and with the face of an uninspired idiot. These sat round and sipped saki and smoked little pipes, and talked to Wild-cherry-bud and Fir-branch, and listened to the grasshopper singing in his cage, whilst more guests arrived, and still more. So that Fir-branch, Wild-cherry-bud, & Co., were full of business, so full indeed that mother Ranunculus, driven to her wits' end, sent out for hired help.

At eleven, when M'Gourley and his companion went out to inspect the golden Shrines, the Tea House of the Tortoise was humming like a bee-hive.

"It's a funny business," said Leslie, as they turned the corner into the street.

"I'm thinkin'," said Mac, "that you'll no find it so funny a beesiness in the end."

CHAPTER VIII

THE SURPRISING STORY OF MOMOTARO—AKUDOGI AND SPOTTED DOG

"I don't care a button," said Leslie, on the third morning of their stay in Nikko. "Danjuro may go be hanged. I'm not going to leave here till I've settled about the kid."

"Ay, ay!" said Mac. "The man who will to Cupar maun to Cupar. I would only imprees upon you this, that time is going and time is money."

"I know; but it won't take more than a few days now. They say they've hunted the whole country round there, and can't find trace of her people."

"Na, and never will. If she has onny real people they won't fash themselves aboot her; girls in Japan are as plentiful as blaeberries in Lorne—you're sadlit with her."

"Well, I want her, that's the truth. I've taken a fancy to her; she's not the sort of thing one picks every day—she and her thunder-cats and dragons."

"I won't say she is not an attractif wee boddie," said Mac, "but think of the future, mon, when she's graun up."

"Bother the future! I'm rich enough to see after her. D'y know, Mac—"

"Weel?"

"I wonder did she come out of those azaleas?"

Mac gave a grunt.

Curiously enough, his point of view had changed, and he was now convinced, or pretended to be convinced, that the treasure trove was a solid body and no bogle.

"Because," went on Leslie, "it may be fact or fancy, but when I picked her up she seemed slipping away into thin air till I kissed her, and then she became solid."

"Imphim," said Mac, using a variation of the sound that was simply stuffed with meanings all uncomplimentary to Leslie's intelligence.

"They used to tell me when I was a kid that babies came out of parsley beds. Well, I'm half inclined to believe the tale has come true at last, and she came out of those azalea bushes. Of course," said Leslie suddenly, and as if apologizing to his own common sense, "I don't really believe it, but I like to fancy it; it's so much nicer than thinking she came into the world the other way."

The prosperity of the Tea House of the Tortoise still continued, people coming from far and near to get a glimpse of the foundling.

Every day Mac and Leslie would take her out for a walk, and she clopped beside them in her little clogs delightfully grave, and seemingly unmindful of the polite following of children that always tailed after them without appearing quite to do so. Children bouncing colored balls, playing hop scotch or what not, yet always with an eye on the child that had come out of the azaleas.

Shopping with Campanula Leslie found to be a new pleasure; a present, no matter what, was received with such deep thankfulness, such quaint expressions of gratitude.

He ordered Mother Ranunculus—requested her, rather—to get a complete new outfit for his charge, everything that money could buy, from tabi to hairpins, from kimonos to clogs. As for toys, she simply wallowed in them: bouncing balls and battledores fell round her as if from the sky, not to mention a doll as big as a baby of three, which she instantly became a mother to, carting it about on her back tucked under her kimono.

The one thing that disturbed Leslie was her seeming indifference to her own strange position. Beyond the bald statement that she had a father, she never referred to that enigmatical gentleman, nor did she grieve, outwardly at least, about her separation from him.

By the end of the week the two Scotchmen and their charge began to be welded into a corporate body—a little quaint family party. It was strange the influence of this child upon these two men whom fate had drawn together from the corners of the earth. Leslie, with newly acquired interest in life, had grown five years younger in mind, and as for Mac, he had grown ten degrees more human. His withered fatherly instincts were awakened—at least they opened one eye—and it was pretty to see him with his gnarled, horny hands and intent, weather-beaten face making chickens for the Lost One out of orange pips.

They would go out, all three, and wander about Nikko and its temples, and they would sit on grassy banks in the gardens of Dai Nichi Do, just as a father and an uncle and niece might sit on seats in Kensington Gardens, and then Leslie and his partner would discuss the future and trade, whilst Campanula played with her doll or bounced a ball.

Here one day, whilst the sun shone on the little lake and the pink and copper maples, the tiny islands and bridges and pagodas, Campanula, weary of play, told, in a sing-song voice and broken manner, the story of Momotaro, otherwise called Peachboy, and his wonderful deeds. She told it standing before them, and striking attitudes suitable to the phases of the tale.

One day, it appears, an old woman found a huge peach, and she was just going to cut it in two with a knife when the peach broke open, and out tumbled a baby. This very surprising thing happened a long time ago, but exactly when Campanula could not possibly say.

Then Peachboy grew up, and every day he grew fatter and stronger, till at last he grew so big that he determined to fight Akudogi, the king of the Ogres, who lived on an island—somewhere. And he started out, said Campanula, with a sword and a bag full of millet dumplings, each with a salted plum in the center, to fight the Ogres.

Here she took from her sleeve a paper of sweets, and gravely presented it to her companions, who each took one. She took one herself, consumed it, and resumed the narrative.

On the way he met a spotted dog, a monkey, and a crow, and to each he gave a dumpling, and they followed him to the attack on Akudogi, the king of the Ogres.

The narrator's voice became deeper in tone, and she spread out her fingers as if in fear.

The crow flew first to the castle of Akudogi and held him in talk, whilst Peachboy, spotted dog, and the monkey, got over the castle wall.

Campanula was now standing before her auditors in a most dramatic attitude, her hands uplifted, the fallen back sleeves of her kimono showing her arms, and her brown eyes full of fear. She did not seem to see either Leslie or M'Gourley. Her eyes were fixed on the frightful Akudogi, and Peachboy, the spotted dog and the monkey, who were about to attack him.

The crow, when he saw that his companions had gained an entrance to the castle, flew away with a laugh, and Akudogi turned and beheld Peachboy and his brave companions. He gnashed his teeth, pulled out his sword, and oh!

Frightened to death with her own imaginations, she rushed with a little shriek into Mac's arms for protection.

"Hauld yourself taegether; I winna let them catch ye! I winna let them catch ye!" cried Mac, as he clasped the perfumed bundle that had flung itself into his arms.

"What's all that she was telling?" asked Leslie, who felt rather jealous that Mac should have been chosen as the harbor of refuge.

"Only a daft tale about ogres an' spotted dogs. She's clean crackit on all sorts of queer beasties. Only last night she told me a tale aboot a rat that played the fiddle an' a tortoise that came to listen, and she told what the tortoise speired an' what the rat made answer, till you could have sworn you heard the rat and the tortoise claverin' taegither."

"Well, hand her over here," said Leslie; "she's not yours." And he took Campanula from Mac and placed her on his knee. "She's mine. I paid ten shillings to that chap with the reed-pipe to whistle her up."

"I'll tell you what," said Mac.

"Well?"

"I'll gi' you ten shullin' for a half share, and pay half the expeenses of her upbringing."

"No, she's mine; you can play with her as much as you like, but I'm going to keep her. She's the jolliest thing I ever struck, and I'm going to stick to her. I saw that policeman Johnnie this morning, and he's quite given up hope of finding her people. They've hunted everywhere. I offered him a fiver to cover the business, but he would not touch the money. He says the chief of police at Tokyo knows you."

"Weel does he know me, seven year and more."

"And he says there's no objection to our taking her along to Nagasaki if you give your bond that she will be looked after, so I was thinking of starting to-morrow."

"Wull you take her with us?"

"I was thinking of leaving her with the 'Tortoise' people till I settle about a place to live in at Nagasaki, and then coming back to fetch her. She'll be all right with them, I suppose?"

"Ay, she'll be right enough," said Mac, and they left the gardens of Dai Nichi Do, and headed for the hostelry.

That night the Areopagus convened itself again, and M'Gourley explained matters. It was necessary that he and his honorable friend should go to Nagasaki, and they proposed that the Lost One should be left behind at the Tea House of the Tortoise, to be kept till called for, warehoused, in short, and, of course, paid for accordingly. Was Madame Ranunculus willing?

Most willing.

A sum of money would be placed in the landlord's hands as guarantee.

Oh, that was perfectly unnecessary!

Still, the Hon. Leslie wished it.

Accordingly, a sum equivalent almost to the value of the Tea House of the Tortoise, was placed in the landlord's hands, who placed it in numerous folds of rice paper, and handed it to his wife, who engulfed it in her kimono.

These matters having been satisfactorily settled, Campanula was led off to bed and dinner was served.

Next morning at eight o'clock two rikshas arrived to take the travelers to the station. The whole of the "Tortoise" folk, Hedgehog San included, came to the front of the house. The cry, "Sayonara—come again quickly," followed them as they swept round the pond and out at the gate, a cry made up of the landlord's croaking basso, the sweet voices of the Mousmès, and Campanula's childish treble.

"She seemed sorrier to part with old Mac than me," thought Leslie as they span along. "Ugh!" He turned his head in disgust from an English tourist in tweeds, who was engaged in kodaking a temple.

In the train, with a pipe in his mouth and M'Gourley opposite to him, he felt as if he had just stepped out of a dream; a dream of sun and splendor, a dream in which figured camellia trees twenty feet high, and the form of the Lost One standing amidst the glory of crimson azaleas.

But another picture obtruded itself upon this pleasant dream.

Away in the mountains not far from Lake Chuzenji, a green thing had been discovered, a thing that had once been a man. Mac had been to view it at the request of the police, but he could not identify it as the body of the Blind One of the Nikko Road. It was green from the chlorophyll of the cryptomerias. In the quaint language of the Japanese police, it was the body of a man whom "the trees had beaten to death."

CHAPTER IX

THE HOUSE OF THE CLOUDS

Danjuro, the curio dealer of Jinrikisha Street, Nagasaki (no relation of Danjuro the actor), was a gentleman of uncertain age, with a face which seemed the relic of a thousand years of debauchery.

It was probably only opium, but the awful weary look with which he swindled you, when you were once in the trap he called his shop, would have given Dante points for the construction of a new circle in his *Inferno*.

He had spent years in China, had Danjuro, hence, perhaps, the expression on his face; also the fact that he did his calculations not by aid of the so-ro-ba, or calculating machine used by the Japanese tradesmen. He did his calculations in his head, and with that far-away look so filled with the poetry of the horrible, he would calculate the difference between the price he had paid for the okimono he was selling you and your offer for it, contrasting them with your own personality, and from these three factors calculating to a nicety how much money he could swindle out of you.

He had a hand in the selling of the Great Tung Jade to the Empress of China, or rather to her ambassador the Mandarin Li, the shadiest transaction that ever emerged from darkness; and could you place end to end the globe trotters swindled and chiseled and fleeced by him, they would reach in a noxious line from London to Newcastle, and maybe further. He had long, polished finger nails that shone like plate glass, and when you entered his establishment he advanced, bowed, and hissed at you by way of welcome.

He was a rogue, yet he was straight in his way. To be a perfect rogue, at least to succeed in the art, you must be straight in some ways. The bandit who betrays his brethren never goes far without a dagger sticking in his back.

M'Gourley had "discovered" Danjuro years ago. M'Gourley had twice come to financial smash, once because of an earthquake, and again in the upheaval caused by the breaking of the Barings. Danjuro had helped him twice, and he had helped Danjuro many times; helped him with his Western craft, Scotch cuteness, and knowledge of Europeans.

In every city of the East, in every city of the world, you will find a fixed Scot always prospering; M'Gourley was a floating Scot. Navigating Japan from end to end, now at Tokyo, now at Kioto, now at Nagasaki, crossing to Corea and pottering about there, meeting brither Scotchmen and helping them in trade speculations, selling, or assisting in the sale, of everything sellable from coals to kakemonos, went M'Gourley, a busy man, but somehow a rather unfortunate one.

Suddenly Japan rose and smashed China, Russia stepped in and robbed her of the pieces, and Japan sat down, drew her kimono round her, and began to think about Russia.

M'Gourley just then (it was some two years before he met Leslie) was on the Lao-Tung peninsula, a black wandering dot, innocuous to governments, one would imagine, as a beetle.

Suddenly M'Gourley returned to Japan, and the day after his return a sheaf of documents addressed by a gentleman named Lessar to a gentleman named Mouravieff was in the hands of the Japanese Council of Elders.

I don't say anything about the transaction at all; it is not for me to take away the characters of my characters. I only know this, that if the Russian Government had caught Mac just then, they, laboring under, perhaps, a fantastically wrong impression, would have done something decidedly unpleasant to him.

At all events, Mac bought a new suit of reach-me-down clothes at a native shop in the Honcho Dori at Yokohama, and got so drunk that three Mousmès had put him to bed, whilst a fourth fanned him, and a fifth played soothing tunes on a moon-fiddle to exorcise the demon; and a piece of priceless gold lacquer presented to Mac by a high official was sold by him to an American week later for five thousand dollars gold coin—gold coin being much more useful than gold lacquer to a man in Mac's way of life.

Thus it came about that Mac was a persona grata with the Japanese Government, and had many little privileges not enjoyed by ordinary Europeans.

Danjuro's shop was situated in Jinriksha Street, a street like a picture slashed out of the "Arabian Nights," a picture that a child had made additions to with a lead pencil and half spoiled.

A bowler hat in Jinriksha Street, for instance, is a thing very much out of place, yet you see many of them, mostly potted down on the back of Japanese heads, and making the wearers both frightful and ridiculous-looking.

Here passes a Mousmè under an umbrella, a figure fashioned seemingly from a rainbow, a figure to bless the eye and make the heart feel glad. Here stumps along a thing that once was a Mousmè, a thing in European dress—alas!

Here you turn from a shop sign in the vernacular, and across the way, over the booth where cakes reposing on myrtle branches are sold, "Englis here is spoke," blasts your sight.

Jinrikisha Street, and for Jinrikisha Street read nearly every other street in seaboard Japan, is a picture, as I have said, spoiled as if by a meddlesome English child.

Danjuro's shop was all open in front so that you could come right in past the bronze stork on the tortoise, past the leaping dragon made of jointed steel, a dragon hard as adamant yet flexible as india-rubber. Then you met Danjuro, and he sank towards the floor and hissed at you by way of welcome. The chief treasures were in the cellar below, but here was quite enough to feast the eye of a not too wise amateur, and make the purse jump in his pocket.

Danjuro had the art of shop-dressing at his finger-ends. Things always looked better in his establishment than they did when fetched home.

People would cry: "Is *that* the Owari vase I bought? Why, *what has happened to it?*"

It would be the same vase, but divorced from its surroundings.

You cannot imagine the effect of a dwarf plum tree in a green tile pot upon a dragon of steel until you see them in juxtaposition, nor the strange difference certain backgrounds make in an Owari vase till you try them. Danjuro was well up in these subtleties, and this knowledge, combined with his own personality, lent an added value to his wares—twenty per cent. at least.

Here in the shop of Danjuro, in a semi-twilight, glimmer demons and beasts in porcelain and bronze. The frightful face of Akudogi shouts at you from the wall, the lotus expands over pools in the silent land of lacquer, and the hundred guinea ivory Mousmè, ten inches high, trips beneath her ivory umbrella, ever on the way to some fanciful pageant that had once existed in her creator's dreams.

Here is a Jap baby, about as big and as round as a tangerine orange, feeding ducks. Here a little box a size larger than a walnut. Open it; inside are seated a man and boy playing some game with dice. The man is holding the dice cup up preparing to cast; in it are the dice, every cube separate and real, and each marked with the proper pips.

In the shop of Danjuro you are gazing, not upon bronzes and lacquers, but upon the mind of Japan, partly made visible. There is here evidence of patience and labor sufficient to conquer the world, beauty enough to charm the world, and ferocity enough to terrify it.

There is nothing so strange on earth as this art that reveals in glimpses the exquisite and the awful, where the lily blossoms and the dragon tramples it under foot.

- 38 -

That baby feeding the ducks, could anything be more laughable or lovable? But do not open the drawers of the cabinet he is standing on: they are filled with ivory obscenities carved with just as loving care.

No, the kakemonos and bronzes that adorn the drawing-rooms of Bayswater and Bedford Park do not disclose the whole of Japanese art. If you don't believe me, then go to Japan and become a friend of Danjuro the curio-dealer, who lives in Jinrikisha Street, in the quaint city of Nagasaki.

"There's no use talking," said Leslie, the second day after his arrival at Nagasaki. "I don't want to live in the European quarter. I want that white house up on the hill there you said was empty, and I want to buy it."

"Weel," said Mac—they were standing in Danjuro's shop consulting—"I'm thinking you want more than it's likely y'll get. You cannot buy the house—rent it, maybe. Stay till I ask Dan."

Dan and he had a consultation, the upshot of which was that the curio-dealer, after a cynical declaration to the effect that anything could be obtained for money, offered his services as an intermediary.

A friend of his, a brother dealer, a Mr. Initogo, or some such name, owned the house up there on the heights; he would probably let it. It was named the House of the Clouds, warranted rainproof and free from ghosts.

Mr. Initogo was fetched from across the way—a gentleman in horn spectacles, who looked as wise as Confucius but was a little bit deaf. After some five minutes' polite bawling on the part of Mac and Danjuro, Mr. Initogo came to understand the matter, and at once declared with a thousand protestations of regret that the thing was impossible.

Why?

Well, he could not allege any specific reason. The House of the Clouds was empty, but he had not considered the matter of letting it. The proposition came as an honorable shock to him.

Then Mac and Danjuro tackled Mr. Initogo, tea was brought forth, and after half an hour's wavering Mr. Initogo began to give in.

He sent for his son, and piloted by the son, the two Scotchmen went off to inspect the House of the Clouds.

They passed up a by-street and then up a steep path, till they came to a gate shadowed by lilac trees. The gate led to a tiny demesne, a long, white, two-storied house, before which lay a grass plot, at the far end of the house some cherry trees, and a space that might be used as a garden.

From the veranda of the House of the Clouds one could look down on Nagasaki and the harbor that pierces the land like a crooked sword. The hum of Jinrikisha Street came up, mixed with the eternal song of the cicalas.

Across the harbor, where the junks and sampans contrasted strangely with the foreign shipping, hills rose up, green near the water, brown further off; over the hills a few white fleecy clouds passed on the light wind. It was the sky of an English summer.

"I like this," said Leslie, turning from the view. "Now let's look at the house."

It was furnished with primrose-colored matting, nothing else, and it was about as substantial as a bandbox. There were two stories connected by a flight of steps without a balustrade, and you could make as many rooms as you liked with sliding panels.

"I'll take it," said Leslie, and they returned to the shop of Danjuro. Mr. Initogo was fetched, and after more wriggling and haggling and tea-drinking and the smoking of tiny pipes, he consented to let the place—the authorities willing.

Mac undertook to make everything right in that respect, though it would cost him a good deal of trouble, as the government have a holy horror of foreigners spreading beyond the allotted quarters; and then a Chinese comprador was obtained, and received orders from Leslie to furnish the place with the necessary futons (he determined to live in the native way), pots, tins, kettles, Mousmès, and a decent cook; also screens and mosquito-nets, plum trees in pots, and everything else that might be necessary for comfort and adornment.

Three days later the comprador appeared at the Nagasaki hotel, where Leslie was staying, and declared that everything was in order—even to the last tea-cup. He had hired servants, made a most advantageous bargain: he had hired a whole family.

"But, bless my soul! I don't want a family," said Leslie. "I only want a cook and a couple of girls."

Just so. This family consisted of a cook—her name was Fir-cone—and three daughters. They would all come together or not at all; he had got them at a bargain. The names of the daughters were: Moon, Plum-blossom, and Snow. Sixteen shillings a month a-piece was the wages they were promised. There was also a cat belonging to this family—

"Oh, well, I'll take them," said Leslie, "and if they don't suit I can get others."

That afternoon, preceded by the comprador and followed by two coolies carrying his luggage he went up to take formal possession, and was received by his new servants all on their knees—the three Mousmès in front and mother Fir-cone in the background.

Next day he started on the long journey to Nikko to fetch Campanula. When he returned with his charge the first person to meet him on the quay was Mac. Mac in a stove pipe hat he had bought cheap and which did not fit him but of which he seemed proud. Campanula instantly recognized Mac with a smile and an attempt to kow-tow before him, which Leslie frustrated, on account of the dirty state of the quay. It was a pretty little incident, and went to the old fellow's heart.

CHAPTER X

OF MOUSMÈS AND OTHER THINGS

Plum-blossom was a Mousmè with a broad face, ever lit by a half smile. Moon was a girl with a serious expression, but gorgeous of dress as any girl of Kioto. Snow looked shrunk—not withered, you understand, fresh as a daisy, in fact; but something had happened in her development: she was preternaturally small, and looked like a Mousmè seen through a diminishing glass.

The three Mousmès and old mother Fir-cone took almost entire possession of Campanula San when she arrived, and Campanula San seemed quite content.

Mixed with her charming childishness there was a philosophical calm that would have done honour to a sage of the Stoic school. Riding on Leslie's shoulder through Nikko, under examination at the Tea House of the Tortoise, playing with Plum-blossom in the veranda of the House of the Clouds, she was just the same. Life was a pageant at which she was an humble spectator, whose duty was to be amiable and submissive, and accept things just as they came.

She did not say this, but she acted it, or rather expressed it in her actions and ways.

Down on the Bund an office had been rented by M'Gourley. He slept there and lived there, ascending occasionally at night to the House of the Clouds to smoke a pipe with his partner and talk business, and give advice on things Japanese, advice often needful enough to the uninitiated Leslie.

House-keeping in Japan is full of surprises. One day, for instance, Leslie met a figure coming from the back part of the premises—a figure like a rag-doll that had spent its life in a coal-scuttle. Interrogated, the figure turned out to be the mother of Moon, and by profession—well, her profession was helping to coal the Canadian Pacific boats.

"But," said Leslie, "it is impossible, for Moon already has a mother whose name is Fir-cone."

He was just going to send for the police when the whole truth came out on the veranda, in the form of Moon herself.

She explained in indifferent English, kneeling as she spoke with the backs of her little hands held upwards to her face, that the comprador had lied; that there was no particular connection between her and her fellow-servants; that the comprador had made a bunch of them just as he might make a bunch of weeds, picking one up here and the other there, and pretending they were all the one family. Why had he done this thing? Who could say? For some dark reason of his own. She said also that her mother was not always as dirty as that, but was going home now to wash. Would Leslie San like to see her washed so that Moon's words might be proved to him true? Leslie San would not.

M'Gourley was had up, and managed to arrange matters without the disruption of the household, which seemed imminent.

M'Gourley mixed a good deal in the affairs of the House of the Clouds. Six months had not passed before the member of the Wee Kirk declared that Campanula should be sent to the missionary day school near the Bund, and brought up a Christian.

Leslie at first demurred. The state of Campanula's mind, as revealed by her in conversations mostly translated by Mac, but often conducted limpingly by Leslie himself (he was beginning to pick up the native), did not argue a good foundation for a structure like the Christian religion.

Her mind, as far as he could get at it, was the mind of a sensitive and cultured lady who was slightly mad—mad on the subject of demons and strange beasts.

Tortoises who talked, storks whose language was the acme of politeness, and toads of polished speech, seemed as real to her as ordinary folk.

Whether the tin-smith, her supposed father, had filled her head with these things, no one can say, but the fact remained that she was a perfect Uncle Remus as far as animal-tale construction was concerned, and had a Mrs. Radcliffe touch in the weird, so that it was a not uncommon thing for her to be marched off to bed, the triumvirate of Mousmès—Moon, Plum-blossom, and Snow—acting as a body-guard to protect her from her own extraordinary fancies.

Then the self-abasement, the absolute self-abasement with which she would kow-tow with both tiny hands backs upward before your august self, and next minute she would be spinning a top on the veranda, or playing just like an ordinary child with Kiku San, a dot about her own size, and only daughter of Mr. Initogo, the landlord.

She had a whole host of baldheaded Pagan friends, male and female, and Leslie, taking a siesta of an afternoon, would hear their clogs rattling on the veranda, or their naked feet pattering in the kitchen, and half fancy himself the proprietor of a kindergarten.

Quaint kites were often to be seen flying above the House of the Clouds, kites shaped like hawks and butterflies, and M'Gourley down in the street below would sometimes glance up and see these evidences of Campanula's existence, and nod his head and say, "A'weel!" and hurry on to Danjuro's to meet him about some perhaps questionable transaction, revolving in his mind the while the question of Campanula's conversion to Christianity.

He was a strange mixture. He would spend a whole morning in trade. That is to say, he would get to the office on the Bund early, do his correspondence and what not with regard to the export of cheap curios, go to the hotel and have a cocktail, and fish round for victims; find some well-to-do stranger and lead him into Danjuro's shop, deliver him up as a dripping roast into Danjuro's hands, receive his commission, and go off and have tiffin. Then as likely as not he would go up to the House of the Clouds and fetch Campanula out for a walk, and buy her toys, or sweets, or flowers.

And once a week or so he would tackle Leslie about the Christianity business, till Leslie at last gave in.

Campanula went to the missionary day school, the prettiest school child in the world under her scarlet umbrella pictured with flying storks.

Leslie went away sometimes for weeks, leaving her in charge of the Mousmès and leaving Mac with instructions to keep an eye on her welfare.

For the first eight months or so of this new life he was amused and interested, the beauty of the country, the quaintness of the people, the new conditions of life, kept him from thinking much about the past or troubling about the future.

Then came reaction. A craving came on him to see England once again, a veritable home-sickness that was not to be denied.

He made a journey to London. He only spent a fortnight there; every one he had known in the past was either gone or dead. He belonged to no club. It was a miserable fortnight, and every day of it Japan called him back.

When he returned, he told himself that he had done with the West for ever. Just as men sometimes tell themselves they have done for ever with sin, folly, or love.

PART TWO
THE MASSACRE OF THE BLUE-BELLS

CHAPTER XI

THE DREAM

The "Jap Rubbish trade" was prospering mildly.

During the first two years it seemed likely to languish and die, but in the third year it woke up, got on its legs, and, to use M'Gourley's phrase, "began to pick a bit." In the fourth year it was bringing Leslie in some two hundred a year, a fair amount considering the capital originally invested in it.

Not that he wanted the money, he kept his interest in the thing just for something to do—a toy business to play with when he was otherwise disengaged.

As for Mac, he was getting rich, not out of the Rubbish trade, but in a manner we will hint at later on.

The House of the Clouds remained unaltered, save for a tiny landscape garden not much bigger than a dining-table which Leslie had laid out for Campanula. It lay beyond the garden walk in front of the veranda, and it had mountains and rivers and savannas of moss, and old oak trees, fierce-looking, but not much bigger than your thumb, and twisted fir trees that reflected themselves gloomily in lakes the size of hand-mirrors, and a Shinto temple about the size of a Buszard's Dundee cake; there were also bridges across the rivers.

The thing had been laid out as a New Year's gift for Campanula, and it had cost Leslie about the price of a Steinway Grand.

Azalea bushes grew right up to it, azaleas bordered the house, and there was a wilderness of azaleas in the open space near the cherry trees.

Crimson azaleas, imported all the way from the azalea valley at Nikko in the very first year of Leslie's residence in Nagasaki. It was a pretty thought, and it had cost a good penny, and caused much grumbling from Mac, and great admiration in Mr. Initogo, who had turned out the most delightful of landlords, a good hand at whist, and most adaptable about repairs. He was a modern Japanese agnostic when he was well, was Mr. Initogo, and a Shinto when he was ill or in trouble; but he was an all-round good landlord at all times.

One bright afternoon Leslie was seated beneath the cherry trees in a deck chair, his hat tilted back, and the pipe he had just been smoking lying on the ground at his feet. He was asleep. Lately he had been suffering from a touch of fever and chills caught on a duck-shooting expedition down the coast; he had been taking opium for it, and now as he sat beneath the cherry trees the opium was troubling his dreams.

Just before dropping off, his eye had fallen on a single azalea blossom that had burst into flame, as if spring had just touched off with her torch the fire of crimson flowers that soon would blaze round the house.

Then he fell asleep, and Opium plucked the crimson blossom, and followed him with it into the land of dreams.

He was in a Hongwanji temple, and there were people there, Europeans seemingly, dressed in European clothes; but though in a specious disguise, they were soon perceived to be not the people of this earth. They had strange and distorted faces, and forms that surely never were made in God's image. One man, who suddenly hid himself behind a screen of lacquer, Leslie could have sworn was made of stone.

Then in great tribulation of spirit he was escaping from the company of these people, passing down a corridor where soft matting took the foot; but something was following him with a hissing sound, a sound such as Danjuro made by way of welcome when you entered his shop. Of a sudden the opium spirit touched the corridor wall with the flower he had been patiently carrying, the Hongwanji temple vanished, and Leslie found himself on the Nikko road.

The valley of azaleas lay before him and the mournful cypress trees, the country where the moving clouds cast their shadows, and the far blue hills beyond.

There was something moving amidst the azaleas. He knew it was a child, but, by some curious and subtle freak of the opium fiend, the child was hidden from him, all but vague glimpses; were it to make itself half visible for a second a phantom azalea bush would come before it, but he could see a tiny white hand busy plucking the crimson blossoms.

Then from somewhere far away through the dream came the mournful toot, toot, of a blind man's reed-pipe. At first it seemed beyond the bend of the road, and then it seemed amidst the azaleas, and then in the wood of cypress trees. It grew more insistent and piercing, and changed subtly into the sound he had once heard on the Nikko road when, sitting with M'Gourley, he had listened to the tune of the blind juggler with the pipe.

As he listened, shuddering, he saw something which he at once knew to be the reason of the music and the soul of the opium drama that was unfolding before him.

A tiny black dot was visible in the sky away over the distant hills. It expanded and grew, dilated as if in response to the enchanted music. And then he saw that it was a bird; a vast bird, larger than an eagle, a ferocious and awful bird, a tragic apparition called up from the lands of night. It poised above the valley, seeming to float and be upborne, not on air, but on the music welling from the wood.

He knew that if he could get to the half-seen child amidst the azaleas he could save it from its fate. But he could make no movement nor utter a sound, but stood paralyzed, watching the tiny white hand plucking the crimson flowers and the Horror above preparing to strike.

The music had now turned to a drone, a sound like the spinning sound of a vast top. The thing in the air circled and span. He knew it was preparing to fall like a thunderbolt.

Then he awoke.

He saw the garden, the cherry trees, the house. Opium land had vanished, but the music remained, ringing in his ears; or was it real?

He sprang to his feet and staggered along the path leading to the gate looking wildly round him and listening. As he came, the sound died off; died and turned to the sound of ordinary life, the hum from the city below, the sound of the wind in the lilac trees, the tune of ceaseless cicalas.

"My God! what a dream!" he muttered as he grasped the gate and stared down the lilac-shadowed path. Then he returned slowly to the seat beneath the cherry trees, and lit a cigarette.

Opium had played a trick upon him like this before. He had taken it first months ago for fever; since then he had taken it occasionally for the slightest ache. He reacted well to it sensually speaking, and found it at once soothing and stimulating. Once before it had pushed him into dreamland, but a dreamland without plot or plan, and unstained by a horror such as he had just witnessed.

He was seated half drowsing, when suddenly some influence made him look up and he saw before him a lovely thing. It was Campanula. She had just come out of the house by way of the veranda, and was approaching him. Campanula, far removed from the child he had carried on his shoulder into Nikko five years ago.

The child had turned into a girl with that rapidity of transformation characteristic of the women of Japan. She was taller than the ordinary Mousmè of fourteen or fifteen; her face, even to Western eyes, was beautiful with a sad and mysterious beauty of its own, and her every movement was graceful as the movement of a bluebell when touched by the wind.

She had ceased to attend the mission school after nearly four years' instruction, during which she had grasped the art of speaking and almost of thinking in English, and was now Leslie's housekeeper, his adopted daughter, and absolute ruler of the small domain known as the House of the Clouds—as far, that is to say, as the household affairs went.

She still retained her childishness of mind, and for all the Christian endeavor of the missionaries, she still retained much of her pristine belief in "things"—things with wings as well as hoofs, things that lived in woods, birds that talked, and beasts that made answer.

Though she could speak English, she never spoke in long sentences, or told a connected tale in that language, always falling back on the vernacular when her imagination was roused, or a long and connected statement had to be made.

She was approaching Leslie now with a porcelain bowl figured with storks in her hand, and a smile upon her face. There was little mat on the ground near his chair, and on this she sat down—kneeling fashion—with the bowl before her.

"See!" said she, producing some things like small gun wads from the sleeve of her kimono, "I bought these to-day to give you pleasure. Oh, so beautiful! Watch!"

She cast one of the ugly discs upon the surface of the water. It lay there for a moment unchanged, and then, as if by magic, began to expand as it sucked up the fluid, and break up, growing bigger and broader till at last on the surface of the water floated three pink-tinted lotus-flowers, a most delicate and perfect resemblance of the real things.

She folded her hands and looked up at him with a happy smile.

"Where did you get them?" asked Leslie.

"M'Gourley San told me of them, he wished to buy them for me—but I bought them for you."

She removed the lotus-flowers and cast another disc on the water.

Leslie watched her. During the last few months Campanula's attitude to him had changed. From a happy, humble, and somewhat heedless thing—a creature that regarded him with affection—an affection of about the same strength as she exhibited for M'Gourley, Sweetbriar San, the cat, and her children schoolmates; she had become a follower of his alone, always striving to please him, forestalling his wants, always happy in his presence, and drooping—unknown to him—when he was away.

The second wad under the influence of the water broke up and began to form the branch of a cherry tree covered with blossom.

"Arashiyama," murmured she, folding her small hands and speaking dreamily, as if communing with herself. Then she sat watching the branch of the cherry tree expanding over the surface of the water.

From the house came a somewhat discordant voice singing a song about a bee and a lilac bough.

It was Pine-breeze singing at her work. Moon, Plum-blossom, and Snow, with their fictitious mother Fir-cone, had vanished from the House of the Clouds two years and more, giving place to Pine-breeze, a miracle of daintiness and prettiness, and two other Mousmès, one "rather old," the cook, Lotus-bud by name, and the other named Cherry-blossom, as pretty as Pine-breeze.

"Listen!" said Campanula, suddenly looking up from the bowl and its contents. "There is some one at the gate."

Leslie half turned.

A man and woman had passed through the gateway shadowed by lilac, a short, stout man dressed in tweed and a tall woman in blue serge.

Leslie could see them only indistinctly from where he sat, and they, not looking in his direction, failed to see him at all.

They were coming up to the veranda when the woman turned to the little picture garden, laughed, and pointed it out to her companion. Then she left the path, stepped gingerly right into the middle of the landscape garden country, and tried to pluck up an oak tree, a gnarled and ancient-looking oak tree eight inches high.

"Who?" asked Campanula, turning from the sight of this outrage with uplifted forefinger.

"They are Foreign Devils," said Leslie using the Chinese idiom. He was very pale, leaning forward in chair. "Look, Campanula! I verily believe she is trying to tear up your mountains to see how they grow. That's what they call in England 'cheek,' Campanula."

CHAPTER XII

THE FOREIGN DEVILS

The female Foreign Devil having failed to uproot the oak, which clung to its native soil with a tenacity highly Japanese, returned to the garden path. And then came the voice of Pine-breeze kow-towing to the strangers, bidding them welcome, and imploring them to make the honorable entrance.

They passed from view into the house, and Leslie rose from his chair.

"Wait here awhile, Campanula," he said, "and then follow me in. I think I know them, but I will go and see."

"Yes," said Campanula.

He walked to the house and kicked his garden shoes off in the veranda, noting the fact that the Foreign Devils had committed the unspeakable outrage of entering with their shoes on.

"*Richard!*" cried the tall woman, advancing to him with outstretched hand as he entered the room where they were. "Why, you've grown!" She spoke as though they had parted yesterday, but her voice had an hysterical quaver, then she presented her cheek to him for a cousinly kiss.

"This is Richard Leslie," said the woman, turning to the little stout man in tweed. "We grew up together; that's why I'm so tall, I suppose. Dick—my husband George. Gracious, Dick, where are your chairs and things? Have you nothing to sit down on?"

"Only the floor," said Leslie, fetching some square cushions and placing them on the matting. "See, this is how it's done," and he sat down on one of the cushions, whilst his companions followed suit.

Jane du Telle, once Jane Deering, was, despite her vivacity and carelessness of manner, evidently in a state of high nervous tension.

Leslie, notwithstanding the years that had passed since their last meeting, saw in her mentally little change. She was the same Jane who had once hacked his shins, when they were boy and girl together, up in Scotland, and then flung herself on his neck in a burst of repentance and tears. Emotional, good-hearted, selfish—giving herself away one moment, but always saved the next by a latent discretion that was to her flighty nature as a gyroscope. The same Jane with whom he had fished for salmon and played at tennis in the past, seated before him now on a floor in Japan, chattering of everything and nothing just in the old familiar way.

"And that's the fellow she has married!" thought he, as he glanced across at George du Telle, a podgy, red-headed little man, a globe-trotting Briton of the most blatant description.

"How did you know I was here?" asked he, after Jane had somewhat talked her hysterical feelings off.

"Mr. Channing told us last night at the hotel. He's a friend of yours. He told us he knew an Englishman named Richard Leslie living in the native fashion, and I asked him if he was good-looking and tall and dark, and he said, 'Yes.' He said you lived at the House of the Clouds—sounds like an address in a dream, doesn't it?—so we took rikshas and came."

She put her hand to her back, where the "floor stitch" had seized her. The floor may be a convenient enough resting-place for a Mousmè who sinks down upon it quite naturally in the likeness of a compressed and joyously colored Z, but for an English woman of five feet eight or more, dressed in a tailor-made gown, and laced in a *corset parfait* it is at first rather difficult.

"I would have got chairs," said Leslie, "if I had known you were coming; but of all the people of the world, you were the last I expected to see. Where did you come from? I mean, how did you strike Nagasaki?"

"We came from Colombo."

"Beastly hole," put in her husband, who was stroking Sweetbriar San, the cat of the establishment, who had just come in to inspect the strangers. "We stayed at the Beach Hotel two nights, and d'you know what they charged us? Just think."

"Don't think," said Jane, who had wriggled into a more comfortable attitude. "Give me that cat, George; and I wish you would try to repress your hotel bills. Dick, I was so sorry to hear the news about your father."

"What news?"

"About his death."

"Well, you were sorrier than I was."

"Oh, Dick! but don't let us talk about it, it's all so sad. And have you been living here in Japan ever since?"

"Ever since."

"Just like this on the floor?"

"Just like this on the floor."

"You must find it rather flat, I should think," said the carroty-headed George.

"Richard," said Jane suddenly, ignoring her husband, "you're not married to a Japanese—or anything—are you?"

"No."

"Do you live here alone?"

"Well, I have three servant girls, and a daughter, if you call that 'alone.'"

"A daughter!" said Jane.

"Yes; and she's Japanese, too."

"Japanese!"

"Yes; I adopted her."

George du Telle snorted, and fortunately at that moment a panel slid back, and Pine-breeze appeared with the tea, followed by Lotus-bud with an hibachi and Cherry-blossom with a heap of tiny plates.

"Are these your—I mean is one of these your—"

"Daughter? No. Turn round, and you will see her,"

Jane was seated with her back to the drawn-back panel that made a doorway on to the veranda. She turned, and there in the sunlit space stood Campanula in her blue kimono, broad scarlet obi, and with a scarlet flower in her hair. Behind her, as a background, lay the picture garden, antique hills, spun-glass torrents, and tiny, twisted fir trees, that looked, oh, so old, and tired of the world, and tormented by the wind.

Campanula went right down on her knees upon the matting, and murmured the usual Japanese welcome.

Now this was a practice that Leslie disliked. He had tried to break her of it, and in the attempt he had come across a strange fact.

Campanula in her heart of hearts was a real child of Old Japan. She might have been a sister to the seven-and-forty Ronins in the time before Osaka was defiled by factory chimneys, and the monastery of Kotoku-in by the presence of Cook's tourists.

She tried honestly to be modern, as it was the wish of Leslie, but in times of emotion, back her intellect would go to Old Japan, and she would act as her ancestors had acted in who knows what lotus-strewn and blossom-scented ages.

"What does she say?" asked Jane, as George du Telle rose to his feet. "Tell me, and ask her to excuse me for not getting up, for when I get up, I'll have to be *pulled* up."

- 54 -

"She is bidding you welcome and at the same time apologizing for the fact of her own miserable existence."

"I accept the apology," said Jane, as Campanula, her devotions over, sank down before the tea-service, and prepared to act as hostess. "Freely and frankly, Dick, I must congratulate you on your taste—she is lovely."

Campanula looked up with a faint, apologetic smile.

"I speak English," she said.

CHAPTER XIII

THE MONASTERY GARDEN

Jane gazed over Nagasaki, the blue water, the green hills, to the blue beyond, and sighed. They were standing near the gate; tea was over, and they were waiting for Campanula, who had gone into the house to make some alteration in her dress before accompanying them "down town."

"Richard," she said, "take us somewhere where we can talk, you and I. I have such a heap of things to ask you and talk about. Twelve years—can it be twelve years since we last saw each other? Did you get my last letter?"

George du Telle was standing near smoking a cigar, and staring at the beautiful view with about the same amount of interest he would have felt had it been a soap advertisement, but she did not lower her voice. She was perfectly frank with the world and her husband.

This frankness carried her far, and enabled her sometimes to skate on ice that would have given under many a woman of half her weight, for it was a genuine frankness, not a thing put on.

She was a person whom women called nice-looking on first acquaintance, and men mentally registered as plain. Tall, pale, with an excellent figure, and gray eyes. A man met her and spoke to her, and found her plain but very jolly, increased the acquaintanceship and found her plainness vanishing, and then, all of a sudden, his foolish soul was caught in a trap.

It was the magic of her lips, perhaps. They formed the true Cupid's bow, full, and seemingly cut by a chisel wielded by a master hand, sensitive and sensuous. Gazing at them one came to understand how in the ancient world tall Troy fell before a kiss.

"Which letter?" asked Leslie, plucking a lilac spray and strewing the ground with the tiny petals.

"The one I wrote six years ago telling you I was married. I sent it care of your father."

"No," said Leslie gloomily. "I have heard from no one for eight years and more. I cut the world, you know—or it cut me rather; but I'll tell you some other time, here's Campanula."

Then they started, Leslie and his companion leading the way.

"Where are you going to take us?" asked Jane, when they had reached the street.

"Through the city to a place I know on a hill," replied Leslie.

He had called four rikshas from the stand, and he gave some directions to the riksha men, and they started.

You cannot imagine the size of Nagasaki till you drive through it in a swift-running riksha, nor the quaintness, nor the terror that causes your heart to fly upwards as your riksha man shaves a baby, not with a razor, but with the off wheel.

Boy babies fighting tops, girls bouncing colored balls, flights of children whose clogs clatter like the dominoes in an Italian restaurant as they pursue each other in some mysterious game—everywhere children, a shifting, colored maze in which the eye gets tangled and lost. Babies, temples, tea-houses, streets upon streets of houses that look as if you could flatten them out with the blows of a shovel, bursts of cherry-blossoms, tripping Mousmès, stone monsters, awful, yet pathetic with the gray of lichen and the green of moss, a courtyard with a twisted fir tree leaning across it, laughter, and the tune of a *chamècen* running through it all, that is the impression that a riksha ride through Nagasaki in spring would leave on the mind, were not the picture blurred by the European element.

Street after street they passed through, and still the mysterious city kept building up streets before them. Leslie had thought of taking his companions to the O Suwa, but he had changed his mind and given other directions to the riksha men.

They passed up a steep incline, dark with fir trees, and drew up at a great gateway consisting of two joists of wood supporting a vast beam, the whole making a figure something in the fashion of the Greek II.

Beyond the gateway lay an inclined path, bordered by cryptomeria trees, leading to the façade of a temple.

"It's a place I sometimes come to," said Leslie, as he helped Jane to descend. "It's quiet, and worth seeing in its way."

Campanula and George du Telle led the way this time, Leslie and his companion leisurely following.

"Come down this path," said Jane, turning to a side alley. "Oh, how pretty! and how mournful too, with those rows of dark trees. Dick, this is not a cemetery you have brought us to?"

"No; it's a Shinto monastery. Few people know it, and it's out of the run of the general sight-seeing bounders."

"Things with kodaks?"

"And without—but see here, Jane."

"Yes?"

"What's your husband?"

"George?"

"Yes, I suppose his name is George. What is he?"

"He's in the wool trade—he's the richest man in the wool trade, they say. He thinks and talks of nothing else but wool. He got off the subject to-day with you for awhile; wasn't he brilliant? But we get on all right together; he has his set, and I have mine."

"What is his set?"

"The very best—I mean the very worst; the poor old Smart Set that every one is always beating as if it were a donkey—which it is," said Jane, taking her seat on the plinth supporting the prancing figure of Ama-ino, fronted across the walk by the equally fantastic figure of Koma-ino, a veritable Lion and Unicorn. "Sit down beside me, Dick, and tell me—"

"Yes?"

"What have you been doing all these years?"

"I—I've been keeping alive—"

"Dick," suddenly broke out Jane, as if she had not been listening, "I have often thought you must have thought me a heartless wretch; but I'm not."

"There is no use in going over the past," he said. "What is done is done, and never can be undone. I can only say that I have never in the past had a friend to stick to me, or a woman to love me, or a father to care for me."

"May it not have been your own fault, Dick? Think for a moment. I don't want to reproach you, but you know how wild you were—you know that was one of the reasons we couldn't get married. Oh, it wasn't 'my heartlessness,' as you told me in your last letter but one. I have heart enough—at least I hope so," said Jane, looking at Koma-ino as if for confirmation, "and I wouldn't have done what I did if you'd been different. Never mind, Dick, cheer up!—buck up! as they used to say in the poor old Smart Set, till the respectable folk took the expression away from them. What've you been doing all these long years, Dick?"

"Oh, I've been in Australia."

"What were you doing there?"

"Curse Australia!" suddenly broke out Leslie, digging his heel in the ground. "Don't speak to me about it; let's talk of something else."

"Well, what are you doing here? I mean, what have you been doing all these years—playing the guitar, or what?"

"I'm a shopman."

"I beg your pardon?"

"I and a man named M'Gourley are in business."

"Two Scotchmen?" sneered Jane.

"Two Scotchmen."

"And what are you selling—paper umbrellas?"

"Yes; and hats and kakemonos, and every other sort of a mono that the European trade will swallow. We export them."

"Then you're a merchant, *not* a shopman," said Jane in a half-angry, half-relieved voice. "I *wish* you would not give me these sort of horrible shocks. I thought at first you were serving in some place behind the counter—"

"Oh, I don't want to make money in business much; I do it more for interest and to have an object in life. I'm well off; my father's money all came to me—he died well off."

"And wasn't it queer?" said Jane. "George is awfully rich, you know; well, directly I was married, old Aunt Keziah died, and every penny of her money came to me. Fifty thousand. No, forty-eight thousand, four hundred and eighty-two pounds, ten and sixpence. It seemed so sweet, the little sixpence following at the end. I sent for it, and had a hole drilled through it, and I always wear it on this bangle—look!"

He looked; there were many things hanging on the bangle. He touched a tiny gold pig swinging by a ring.

"Good heavens!"

"*You* gave me that," said Jane, "and I've never parted with it."

"What's this?" said he, fingering a cabalistic-looking blue stone.

"That's an inkh, I think; I'm not sure of the name. It's lucky, or supposed to be."

"Who gave it to you?"

"A boy at Cairo last winter."

"How old was he?"

"Oh, about twenty."

"And this?" said Leslie, picking out another charm in the form of a heart.

"Look here," said Jane, pulling her wrist away, "I don't want to waste time like this, I want you to tell me more about yourself; I want you to tell me about that child Campanula. *Why* did you adopt her?"

"I found her on the road going to Nikko."

"Where's that?"

"It's away up in Shimotsuke, beyond Tokyo. I and M'Gourley were on the tramp. We were sitting by the roadside resting, when a blind man came along. He was half mad, and talked wild. Said he was a juggler, and offered to fetch devils out of a wood near by, if we gave him gold."

"Why didn't you try him?" said Jane in an interested voice.

"I did try him," said Leslie; "gave him some money. He made a circle in the dust, with signs round the rim of it, told us not to touch it or come near it, got into the middle of it, and fetched out a reed-pipe. Then he began to play a tune that would make you shiver to hear, and things croaked in the wood."

"Go on," said Jane shivering pleasantly.

"I took my walking-stick and made a mark in the dust just near his foot. I touched his heel by accident, and—whew!"

"Yes?"

"He went off like a rocket; bounded out of the circle, rushed this way and that, knocking against trees and striking right and left with his stick, as if dogs were about him. He got round the bend of the road and vanished. We were pretty much astonished, but that wasn't the end of it. In front of us was a valley of the most beautiful crimson azaleas."

"Wait a moment, Dick; you're a very bad story-teller. You should always stage your characters: you should have described the azaleas first and the scenery. Well, go on."

"Bother the azaleas!" said Dick. They were fast getting into the old boy-and-girl way of talking to each other, a somewhat dangerous language at thirty. "It doesn't matter whether they come in first or last. Where was I? Oh yes. Mac suddenly said: 'Look there!' I looked, and there sure enough was a child amidst the azaleas. She hadn't been there a few seconds before, and Mac would have it that she had been 'fetched'; it was a pretty wild country and no houses around, and there she was, just as if she had stepped out of a house, plucking away at the azalea blossoms for all she was worth, a tiny dot in a blue kimono and scarlet obi. I stole up behind her."

"I'd have caught her up and kissed her."

"Just what I did, in fact; and it may have been fancy, but she seemed slipping through my fingers like—grease till I kissed her, and she became solid."

"There's one thing, Dick, you'll never make a poet. Well, go on; it's awfully interesting."

"We carried her off to Nikko. No parents could be found to own her, so I adopted her."

"What became of the juggler?"

"That was a funny thing. As we turned the bend of the road we saw him away up in a gorge of the hills. He was still running for all he was worth, beating about him with his stick as if hitting off devils, and dashing himself against trees in a quite regardless manner."

"How awful!"

"Well, frankly, it was, and it had a sequel, for his dead body was found miles away some days after, and the Japanese police said the trees had beaten him to death, which they practically had."

"But, Dick, what was the meaning of it?"

"Who knows! When I touched him on the heel perhaps he may have thought it was a devil seizing him, and his imagination did the rest. Mac thinks, or, at least, he once thought—"

"Yes?"

"That there was something developing in the wood, something bad; that Campanula's ghost was wandering in the wood; that when I made the mark I did inside the circle, the bad thing was flung out of the developing medium and Campanula's ghost sucked into it, and so she became materialized."

"And the bad thing went for the juggler man?"

"It and perhaps others."

"I never heard anything half so horrible, if it's true."
"It's true enough. I was forgetting it almost, but I had a horrid dream to-day that brought it all back. I was sitting in the garden smoking and I dropped off to sleep; and I heard the sound of that beast's pipe, and I saw the place on the Nikko road, and there was a child amongst the flowers. Then a frightful bird came along and was going to attack the child, and I awoke—it was just before you came."
"Dick, what was the mark you made on the road?"
"The sign of the cross," said Leslie.
Jane was silent for a moment then—

CHAPTER XIV

NAGASAKI BY NIGHT

"I wish you wouldn't tell me stories like that," she suddenly broke out. "I'll be dreaming about it all to-night." She shuddered, and gazed at Koma-ino. "Japan seems a horribly creepy sort of place; I think I'll make George come away to-morrow."

"One side of it," said Leslie, "is simply crawling; you have no idea, and I who have lived here five years have only a glimmering of the mind of the people. Do you know what I think?"

"Yes?"

"I think that in the sleeves of their kimonos—I mean their frock coats, for they've put off their kimonos for a while for business purposes—they are simply laughing at us."

"At whom?"

"At the English—at Europe."

"Like their impudence!"

"Perhaps it's impudence, perhaps not, anyhow—I distrust them—"

"Dick," said his companion, "look! It's getting dusk: let's go and look for George and your 'adoptive daughter.' Mercy! What's that!"

A deep hum filled the air; it seemed to come at first from the statue of Koma-ino—a soul-disturbing hum that deepened and swelled and then leapt, leapt into a deafening roar that rushed over Nagasaki, to die on the distant sea.

Jane clung to her companion like a child, hugged him as a child might hug a nurse; her straw hat was pushed sideways, and he found his face buried in the masses of her perfumed hair. His arm had slipped round her waist, her arm was over his shoulder, and her fingers pressing his neck; for a moment he felt as if he were absorbing her being—drinking her.

Then the sound died away.

"*What* was it?" gasped she, pushing away from him and gazing at him with a white, drawn face. "Why, you seem half dazed; you were more frightened than I. Dick, what was it?"

"I'm all right," said Leslie, in the voice of a man waking from the effect of an opiate. "I wasn't frightened. It was only the big gong of the monastery; I've heard it lots of times."

"Then why couldn't you have told me?" cried Jane, flying from fright to fury. "Think what it must have looked like, you hugging me like that." She sprang to her feet. "You bring me here and tell me ghost stories, and frighten me to death with gongs and things, and then—I believe you're half a Japanese already, you've grown so horrid."

"There wasn't any one to see," said Leslie, rising to his feet. "And talking about hugging—"

"I don't want to talk about hugging—talk about hugging! Do you fancy yourself on Hampstead Heath? Come, let us find George. I want something common-place after all this."

They found George and Campanula—the most strangely matched pair in the world—waiting for them at the gates.

"You'll come and dine with us at the hotel, won't you?" asked Jane as they got into the rikshas.

"I'll come right enough," said Leslie. "Wait, please."

He went to Campanula's riksha and asked her, but she prayed to be honorably excused—she had a headache.

She passed her hand across her forehead as if in confirmation of her words. Leslie tucked the riksha blanket round her knees, and explained to the Du Telles, and they started.

The quaint city they had come through had changed to a quainter city still. Night had blotted out the traces of Europe on Nagasaki—at least, in the purely native streets. All sorts of strange little trades that sleep in the daytime had awakened with the dusk. Things queer in the daytime were now mysterious, and things common, quaint. The fish shop, with its huge paper lantern, besides the fish and the sea-weed on its slabs, disposed of dreams which it flung away gratis to the passing traveler in the running riksha, and the booth of the sandal merchant, with the tiny potted rose tree in front of the wares, became at once an apology and atonement for all the commonplace villainy condensed in the word "shop."

Mousmès passed, now half Mousmès, half glowworms, each bearing a colored lantern on the end of a little stick; and then the shadows half lit by lamp-light, where a cherry tree was attempting to peep into the street: the light of lamps glimmering through paper shutters, the light of lanterns swinging in the wind—red, blue, white, and yellow, some pictured with chrysanthemums; the stork that stands so boldly forth in Japanese pictures but is nearly gone from Japan, cherry-blossoms, and fish that seem swimming vigorously in a bowl of water lambent and green; and then the sounds, ten *chamècens* for one in the day. The riksha whisks by a booth, whence comes the squalling of cats—seemingly. It is the gaku, Japanese poetry set to music and flung into the lamp-lit street to make things stranger, and heighten, if possible, the charm. At the corner of the by-street leading to the House of the Clouds they met Pine-breeze simply laden with all sorts of weird and wonderful paper boxes, and lighting herself on her way with a lantern pictured with a cuttle-fish and carried on the end of a short bamboo rod. She had been marketing. It was a fortunate meeting, for she could escort Campanula home.

CHAPTER XV

M'GOURLEY'S LOVE AFFAIR

Following Pine-breeze, who went before her like a fantastically colored glowworm, Campanula ascended to the house.

As she stepped onto the veranda she heard the voice of M'Gourley San addressing Lotus-bed, and asking when she thought Leslie San would be back. Mac's elastic-side boots were in the veranda, and his gamp was propped against the wall.

He was sitting on the floor smoking a pipe and reading the *Japan Mail* through a pair of spectacles when Campanula entered.

Mac often came up of nights like this. He was a vivid Radical, and Leslie was a hide-bound Conservative, so they had a splendid time together when they got on politics; or they would play chess, or Mr. Initogo would drop in and they would have a rubber of dummy whist.

But what Mac really came for, though he scarcely knew it himself, was Campanula.

Campanula was a lot to Mac; much more than one can express in prose, and M'Gourley is scarcely the figure to make a ballad of. Yet the poem was there round about him, unsung, unuttered, unguessed by any one, least of all by himself.

When he had made chickens out of orange-pips for her at Nikko, she just as cunningly had made him her slave.

She had taken this dull, hard-grained, and shady old business man into a byway, of life, and made him spin tops and fly kites. She had made him admire flowers and listen to fairy tales, and all as naturally and as peacefully as though these things had been matters of everyday occurrence with him the whole long length of his arid life.

"*Einst, O wunder!*"—that ballad might have been inspired by Mac—had the writer ever met him in business or seen him in the flesh.

"Hech!" said Mac. "There you are; and where have you been trapsing to this hour of the evening?"

Campanula explained that Leslie had met friends, and that he had gone to dine with them at the hotel.

"Wonder who they can be?" soliloquized Mac, as Campanula clapped her little hands together for Pine-breeze to bring refreshments. "Some people he has picked up at the hotel, maybe."

They sat opposite to each other on the matting, this strangely assorted pair. A panel in the front was open, for the night was warm, and the lamplight fell on the veranda and the garden path beyond.

And they ate salted plums and crystallized prawns, soup with seaweed in it, and rice with fish sauce, whilst the perfume of the cherry blossoms stole in from the night outside, and the twang of a *chamècen* came from somewhere in the mysterious depths of the house.

It was Lotus-bud relieving her soul with music, mournful as the sound of the wind blowing over the wet fields of millet in the rainy weather.

The things having been removed, Campanula brought forth a chess-board, which she laid on the matting before Mac.

He had taught her chess, and had found her an apt pupil, a veritable Zukertort, a female Nogi, who attacked his positions with her ivory army, stormed his fortifications, and put him to rout when she chose.

Yet he often won. She would make amazing blunders just in time to save him from defeat, and Mac would chuckle and say—

"There you are, there you are—thrown a pawn away that might have given you back your queen in two more moves. Never mind, you're getting on; I'll noat say ye aren't im—" long pause—"proving. Check—and how's that for mate?"

Then Campanula would throw her hands up in assumed horror at her own stupidity, and Mac would chuckle over his own supposed cleverness, and all would be harmony and peace.

To-night, however, Campanula's mind was somewhat astray, and the chess-player who lived in her brain took advantage of the fact, and beat Mac thoroughly in the course of a dozen moves.

"I'm getting auld," said Mac testily. "Here, put the things away. Na, na, I'll play no more the night."

He lit his pipe at the tobacco-mono and moodily smoked it. He could not bear being beaten at chess, and now he looked as if he would be sour for the whole evening.

She reached for a long-necked *chamècen* that lay near her on the matting, and tuned it, striking a few somber notes.

"Ay, sing us something," said Mac, and as the night wind sighed and the cherry blossoms filled the room with their faint, faint fragrance, Campanula, her eyes fixed across illimitable distance, sang in a voice like the ripple of a mountain brook, a song telling of the Miakodori, and the sunlit slopes of

Maruyama, where the great old Gion cherry tree blooms at the foot of Yaamis lane. And then an old love-song strayed in from the night and was caught by the strings of the *chamècen* and made articulate by her voice.

It told the fate of a maiden named Pine-bough, who lived by the sea at Hamada where the foam and the sand are as snow.

She loved a noble, this maiden named Pine-bough—you can guess the rest. Mac listened, soothed; it was the case of David and Saul over again—a very inferior sort of Saul, it is true.

"Now," said the Charmed One as the rafters absorbed the last echoes of the fate of Pine-bough, "tell us a story."

Campanula, with the *chamècen* lying across her lap, knitted her brows in thought. She was evidently pursuing strange beasts across the fields of Fancy, and undetermined as to which she would mark down and serve up to her guest. Then she solved the matter by suddenly clearing her brow and telling a tale without any beasts in it at all.

"There is a garden," declared Campanula, "where every one may enter; the Mikado himself goes there, and the riksha man, the Mousmè and the Mousko, Bo Chan, and Kiku San. Even Campanula herself, lowly as she is, may enter there. And there the Mousko pulls the beard of the Emperor unafraid, and the riksha man forgets his riksha and drinks tea at the tea houses, where no money is paid and no money is asked for."

"What's this garden you're telling me of?" demanded Mac, his business instincts and common sense in arms at the latter statement.

"It is the garden of sleep," answered Campanula cunningly. She had been waiting for the question and now she paused, gently plucking a string of the *chamècen*, filling the air with a faint throbbing sound as if to summon around her the tale-bearers of the night.

"Here in the garden of sleep," pursued the dreamy voice, as the vibrations died away, "every tree bears a lighted lantern swinging in the wind and painting the grass beneath with its color—red lanterns painted with storks, and blue lanterns pictured with the blossoms of the cherry; lanterns on which dragons fly pursuing each other, and lanterns disported upon by my lord the Bat.

"A wanderer in the garden has but to pluck a lantern from a tree, and his dreams will at once turn in a happy direction, and by the light of the lantern he will see before him the object of his desire, be it what it may."

"I'll remember that," said Mac grimly, "next time I find myself there."

"One has no memory there," said Campanula, "and few people know of the secret of that place, else every one would be happy in their dreams.

"One night entered the garden Taro San, a child no higher than one's knee. He was the son of a tea-house keeper, and he had plucked a glowworm from a bush, by which feeble light he was lighting himself through the darkness of the garden.

"All at once he found himself beneath a tree, from the lowest branch of which swung a huge lantern of wistaria-blue.

"It was the lantern of Spring, and the painted butterflies upon it, by some magic, moved their wings in flight, yet remained always in the same place, and the painted cherry-blossoms upon it waved in some magic wind, yet never faded or lost a petal, and the bird upon it pursuing the dragon fly was always gaining upon the dragon fly, yet the dragon fly, oh mystery! always outstripped the bird."

Campanula paused in thought, and a faintly plucked string of the *chamècen* filled the air with the hum of the dragon fly's wings as it flew by reed and iris, by mere and pond, by the unblown lotus and the blue of the river in the country of eternal spring.

"O Taro San," continued the story-teller, "gazing up and beholding this fair thing, strove to reach it, and failing, he began to weep.

"Now, there was passing by at that moment the Daimiyo of his province, and the great lord walked with his gaze fixed upon the ground overcome as he was by the reverie of sleep; but hearing the sound of Taro San weeping, he paused and asked the child what ailed him, and hearing the trouble, he lifted him upon his shoulder; and Taro San grasped the lantern and waved it in the air and laughed, for its light showed him a pleasant path beset with roses and leading to a sea, blue as the sea of Harima, and in the path stood a little girl plucking the amber and crimson flowers.

"Taro cried out to the Daimiyo to take him to the little girl, but the Daimiyo did not heed, for to him the lantern had shown Osaka Castle stormed by knights in armor, and the spears of the Samurai all bent towards its walls under a roof of flying arrows. Towards this sight he ran, and Taro dropping the lantern, it went out, and the Daimiyo awoke in his palace and Taro awoke in the tea house upon the futon, where he slept beside his father.

"Another night stood Taro beneath the lantern which hung beyond his reach, but a beggar man who chanced to pass lifting him upon his shoulder, the child seized the lantern and waved it in the air, and instantly before him appeared the flower-set path and the form of the Mousmè, more beautiful now and attired in a kimono of palest amber embroidered with silver bats.

"But the beggar man saw nothing but a purse of silver lying before him on the ground, and, stooping to pick it up, Taro fell from his shoulder, the lantern went out, and the beggar man awoke by the roadside where he had fallen asleep, and Taro on the futon beside his father.

"Many times did Taro stand beneath the lantern of spring and many people raised him towards it, but never one of them saw what Taro saw, all their dreams being of things other than flowers and the time of spring.

"One night," resumed Campanula after a pause, "Taro entered the garden, and beneath the lantern there stood a child, and the child implored him to lift him upon his shoulder, and being there the child seized the lantern and laughed aloud with pleasure at the vision of the roses, and the Mousmè, and the sea. But Taro saw nothing of this. He only saw a tea house where customers were waiting to be served, for Taro," said Campanula, "Had now grown up, and was a man."

She finished her little tale with three mournful notes drawn from the bass string of the *chamècen*.

"Humph!" said Mac.

He tapped the ashes out of his pipe into the little receptacle of the tobacco-mono, refilled it, and lit it with a glowing ember.

Whilst he was thus engaged, Campanula rose and went to the open panel space leading on to the veranda. He heard her addressing some one in her low, sweet voice, then there was a pause, then she spoke again as if in answer to some remark, then she returned.

"Blind man," said Campanula, putting the *chamècen* away.

"I heard nobody," said Mac, looking up as he finished lighting his pipe. "What did you say? Blind man? Was it he you were speaking to?"

"Yes; he said he had come from a great way, and he looked oh, so ugly and tired! He has gone to the back entrance, and they will give him food."

"It's these blessed paper houses," said Mac.

"They either swallow a sound or magnify it, so's you can't hear yourself speak if a man sneezes in the next room."

He smoked for a while, and then rose to go.

"There!" said Campanula, as she too rose. "He's gone away again down the path towards the gate."

"I'll just follow him," said Mac, "and see what he's like."

He bade Campanula good night and departed.

The gate was closed, and there was no one on the garden path; no one on the hill path either, he found as he descended it slowly, peering through the gloom before him.

"It's dom queer!" muttered Mac to himself as he reached the street. "I'd have staked my life she was talking to herself."

He felt vaguely uneasy, and thought of returning. Then he decided not. The path looked gloomy and mysterious viewed from down below, and its descent without meeting any one had already given him a slight attack of the "creeps."

CHAPTER XVI

THE PHILOSOPHY OF EVIL

Dinner was served in the Du Telles' private room. Channing dined with them—the man who had informed Jane of Leslie's whereabouts—a young, clean shaven man, member of the Shanghai Jockey Club and practically head of the great silk firm of Channing, Matheson & Co.

At dessert Jane asked Leslie's permission to tell of Campanula's finding. Leslie at first demurred. No one knew anything about it except the far-away folk in Nikko and the secretive Japanese police. It seemed scarcely fair to Campanula to give the tale away, but at last he consented, for George du Telle had eaten and drunk himself into a state of torpor. He was staring at a pineapple before him with a flushed face, from which protruded a great cigar, and as for Channing he was off to Shanghai next day. So Jane told the story, and Channing listened.

"Well, what do you think?" said Jane when she had finished her tale.

"I never think about these matters," said Channing, "I simply accept them. My dear lady, were you to live a long time in the East you would come to believe in things that Western people would rank as nursery tales. The Tokyo fire-walkers can walk barefoot over a bed of live charcoal as thick as a mattress. I have seen them. How do they do it? I don't know.

"It is very curious how the Western people, Christians, and so forth, treat the unknown. They look upon it as the unknowable. The Easterns don't. I had a missionary man in at my office the other day over at Shanghai subscription hunting. I gave him what he wanted, and then, without scarcely saying 'Thank you,' he asked me did I believe in God. I asked him did he believe in the devil. He said 'Yes.' I asked him did he believe in devils, and he said 'No.' I asked him did he believe in the Bible. He said 'Yes.' Then I recalled to his mind the story of the Gadarene swine, and his reply was that times are changed since then. Then I suppose, I said, all the devils are dead? He walked away in a huff—with my check in his pocket, though.

"Now the juggler man"—turning to Leslie—"may have been chivied to death by devils just as the Gadarene swine were chased into the sea—who knows?

"Of course it may have been that his madness, if he were mad, took an acute turn, who knows? But I have lived a good time in the East, and I am very well assured of this, that there are men here hand in glove with evil. I have seen things done in China, and for money too, that could not possibly have been done by trickery, and could not, I think, have been done by permission of the powers of Good. I'm not what you call a Christian, and what's more,

I think the Christian religion has done a great deal of harm—not to speak of other what you call 'religions'—Am I wearying you, Mrs. du Telle?"

"Not in the least; please go on."

"In this way. It has robbed us of our terror of evil. It paints a vague devil that no man really believes in. Now take that much-read book, 'The Sorrows of Satan,' where the Devil sits down and plays the piano and sings a song."

"I thought it was a guitar he played," said Jane.

"Well, a guitar; it's all the same. People read that with a grave face. He's quite a good sort and so forth." Channing paused for a moment and gazed reflectively at the wine in his glass, took a sip and went on: "Don't you think the thousands of people who read that stuff, and admire it, must have lost all sense of the horrible thing that evil is? The sense that evil is a reality, a thing to fill us with the wildest horror if one could only appreciate it, a very real thing, and a very determined thing, and a thing all black; yet we get people playing in fancy with, and even laughing about, this horror. And writers painting the cuttle-fish center of it as a semi-sentimental idiot capable of assuming evening clothes and talking twaddle, or criticizing plays as he does in Satan Montgomery's poem. We don't play with a thing we loathe even in fancy. But we—I mean Christians—play with the idea of the devil as if it were a poodle dog. The truth is that Christians don't fear the Power of Evil, they fear the Power of Good. They praise him, propitiate and worship him in a most fulsome manner, and say they love him. I tell you this for a fact that no man can love good who does not abhor evil, and you can't abhor a thing that you play with."

"Do you abhor evil, Mr. Channing?" asked Jane.

"Honestly, I do. Any one with eyes and the capacity for thought who lives in China *must*."

"Then you must love good?"

"One does not 'love' the sun, one worships it, so to speak—but this is all very strange my talking like this; my business in life is mainly silk and racehorses."

"'Scuse me," said George du Telle, who was swaying slightly in his chair, the gone-out cigar still stuck in the side of his mouth, his face bulged and red, and his eye a fixity. "'Scuse me."

"One moment, George—Well, I think, Mr. Channing, there are worse Christians in the world than you are."

"Perhaps there are worse men, but I don't claim to be a Christian. Only a man who recognizes fearfully the existence of evil as well as good."

"'Scuse me," said George du Telle, speaking loudly now as if he were calling a servant or railway porter. "I'm not going to have this sort of thing at my table. *I'm* a Christian, brought up a Christian, die one. 'M not going to—"

"George!" said his wife in a mild voice, but a voice very steady and full of command.

The Christian, who had raised himself in his chair, subsided.

Jane rose from the table.

"Shall we go into the drawing-room and have some music?" she said. "You sing, Dick—or used to."

As they passed to the drawing-room she said to Channing: "Did I tell you the mark my cousin Dick made—you know what I mean—was the Christian emblem?"

"My dear lady," said Channing, "I especially dread hurting another person's religious feelings, and I, what am I? Just a man who thinks his own thoughts, but—"

"Well?"

"Well, if there were anything in it at all, may it not be that the cause of the disturbance was the fact that he touched him?"

"How is that?"

"You have never touched the wire in connection with a running dynamo?"

"No."

"No," said Channing, "for if you had you would not be here. The metaphor is a bad one. I only mean to say that the touch of a stick or a hand may disturb the play of great forces with most surprising results."

- 73 -

CHAPTER XVII

THE HOUSE BY NIGHT

It was late when Leslie left the hotel. The moon was rising over Nagasaki, and he required no lamp to light him up the hill path leading to the house.

In the veranda he sat down to rest a moment and pull off his boots. The landscape garden, looking very antique in the moonlight, lay before him, the moon lighting its tiny hills and melancholy groves with the same particular care that presently he would bestow on the forests of Scindia and the Himalayas. On one of its verdurous swards lay a mark. It was the mark of Jane du Telle's footstep imprinted on Campanula's garden.

He sat for a while in thought, then he unlatched a panel with a sort of gridiron-shaped key, then he searched in his pocket for matches, and found he had none.

Determining to grope his way up and go to bed by moonlight, he closed and fastened the panel, leaving himself in darkness, caught his toe against an hibachi, left as if on purpose for him to tumble over, swore, knocked himself against a screen, which fell crash on Sweetbriar San, the household cat, who had once made part of the Fir-cone, Plum-blossom, Moon, and Snow ministry, and the intelligent animal, conceiving that robbers had entered, rushed wildly round and round in the dark till a panel slid back revealing Pine-breeze with a wan and weary smile on her face, and an andon or night lantern in her hand. She handed Leslie a candle and box of matches, and, still smiling, slid back, closing the panel as she went, like a figure in a trick toy, Sweetbriar San bristling and glowering on her shoulder like a fiend.

The upper part of the House of the Clouds was divided by panels into a passage and three rooms. One for Leslie, one for the Mousmès, and the third for Campanula.

Pine-breeze, with her arm full of towels, or what not, would often come into Leslie's bedroom through the wall. He might be in his bath, he might be—anything, it was all the same to Pine-Breeze, she was thinking of her duties, not of him.

One night, long ago, he had awakened in the arms of Mother Fir-cone, who was jibbering with fright. There was a mosquito-net between them, for she had rushed through the wall, and literally flung herself upon him, tearing the mosquito-net from its attachments. I do not wonder at her fright. Also San was in eruption, and a fearful earthquake was roaring and billowing under Nagasaki.

Several times had the Mousmès rushed into his room all clinging together, and crying "Dorobo!" (Robbers). Robbers had tried to burgle the house twice, in fact. He had shot one the second time, and they never came again. Yet he always slept with a Smith and Wesson convenient, for a Japanese robber is a business man, without a heart, but with a desire for plunder keen as the edge of a sword.

Leslie's bedroom was a very bare apartment, furnished mostly with a nothing. A futon and pile of pillows—he had tried the makura or Japanese pillow, but given it up in disgust—under a mosquito-net, a wash-stand, a stick-rack, and some pegs to hang clothes on, constituted the remainder of the furniture. The window was a wide open space crossed by lattice slats, through which the moon was now shining, her light partly intercepted by the dance of a cherry bough waving in the wind.

Leslie undressed and got into bed. Seen through the blue gauze of a mosquito-net, the room had a character all its own.

The House of the Clouds by night was not the place for a person afflicted with insomnia. There were so many noises only waiting to tell strange tales to the strained ear. Tales of mystery and exaggeration. Lying awake you would hear some one leaning close against the attenuated house wall; it was the wind. And now, a scratching sound as of a panther trying to commit a burglary; it was the wind; and now a whisper like the whisper of a lover to his mistress—or maybe of a robber to his mate; it was the wind.

Then the owl sitting on the roof, staring with saucer eyes at the moon, would give one low, whistling cry, and his mate beyond somewhere, would make cautious answer.

Then "tap, tap, tap." It would be the wind—making the skeleton finger of a dead Samurai out of a loose lattice.

Then a thunder of cats and a yell on the veranda roof, and the drowsy one, just off to goblin land with the dead Samurai, would be brought up all standing, and half rise for a boot, or a boot-jack, or anything hurlable, and sink back with a sigh, remembering that he was in Japan.

The wind played upon the House of the Clouds just as a maestro plays on a fiddle, but with a more distressing result. Sometimes of an autumn or winter night you might have sworn the place was surrounded by a company of old Japanese ghosts escaped from the clutches of Emma O[1] and requestful of succor and safety.

[Footnote 1: The Guardian of the Buddhistic hells.]

Leslie could not sleep. This eruption of his past into the present disturbed him deeply.

He had been getting acclimatized, losing little by little that horrible sense of exile and home-sickness that had driven him once across half the world to London, and now it was all coming back.

And she was married to that little beast, and, worst of all, she seemed content.

For eight years he had looked upon her as a thing dead to him, and now she had returned with sevenfold power, for she brought the past with her. The golden past, golden despite that dour father, Colonel Leslie of Glenbruach, that just man unacquainted with folly. She brought the river in spate and the leaping salmon, the heather-scented wind from the purple hills, Glenbruach in the midst of a world of snow, the ripple of the mountain burn and the faint reek of peat.

Worse than all these, she brought herself. She was the same spiritually and mentally as the slim girl of long ago—a slip of a girl straight as a wand and as full of laughter and movement and brightness as a mountain brook.

But materially she had vastly altered. She was now a woman, divinely formed, a creature appealing to every sensual fiber in a man's nature.

And George du Telle owned all this!

Leslie, I daresay you have perceived, was a man who did not take what one may call a dry-light view of things, past or present, when they had relation to himself; as a matter of fact, he saw the shortcomings of others tremendously clearly. The shortcomings of his father, of Bloomfield the lawyer, of the Sydney bar loafers, of Danjuro the curio dealer, and of poor old sinful, grubbing M'Gourley—too clearly, in fact.

His own shortcomings he acknowledged by word of mouth. He knew they were there, just as a merchant knows a bale of damaged and unsaleable goods is in his cellar, but he did not go down and rake them out and examine them carefully.

No one ever had cared for him, he said, but he never asked himself if he ever had permitted any one to care for him. With this outlook on life, a semi-poetical nature, and passions that slept long and deeply only to awake rejuvenated and with the strength of demons, he might before this have gone entirely to the devil, only for a lodger he had.

An old Scotch ancestor lived with him. This "pairson," who had once worn a long upper lip and had been a writer to the signet, a just, hard, God-fearing, and straight man, had a chamber in a convolution of Leslie's brain, where he sat—he, or his attenuated personality—twiddling his thumbs like a night watchman and waiting for alarms.

It was this gentleman who had saved his descendant from the weak man's form of suicide—drink.

He now came out in his old carpet slippers and read his descendant a lecture on the text: "Thou shalt not lust after another man's wife."

And he spoke hard and strong, taking almost entirely the "wumman's" side of the question; pointing out that society, as we know it, imperfect as it may be, is ruled by a number of laws whose aim is the common weal and the individual's comfort and happiness.

He pointed out that the life of a "wumman" is composed, not of grand passions and Italian opera scenes, but of a hundred thousand trifles, each one insignificant enough, yet each helping to form that grand masterpiece, a pure woman's life.

That a woman might be pure in mind, even if married to a "red-headed runt" like George du Telle. That if that was so she was a happy woman, and that if a man loved her, loved he never so madly, it would be a strange expression of that love to blast her happiness, and soil her soul.

It would not be love, but lust—the passion of those devils which Mr. Channing had hinted at that evening, those people of the night who slumber not nor sleep.

Having finished, he went into his chamber and shut the door.

And Leslie lay reflecting on his words, also on the words of Channing.

Evil made manifest. The face of the creature on the Nikko road came before his mental eye. That was evil made manifest. He had seen the thing. He had known the devil by hearsay since a child. He had heard the "Deevil" thundered at from Scotch pulpits, tracts about the devil had been put into his hand; he had heard people make laughing remarks about him: he was so familiar with the vague personality called Satan that he felt no interest in him, neither interest nor aversion. Never a shudder.

But that thing in the sky of the opium dream, the music that had brought it—that, indeed, was evil painted by the hand of an artist; worth all the sermons ever thundered from pulpits, all the tracts ever printed.

Then his weary brain grew drowsy, and there strayed across it the fair figure of the Lost One, the very antithesis of all things evil.

Only last night before going to bed she had murmured a story half to herself, half to him, with her eyes fixed on the glowing embers of the hibachi, and he retold it to himself now to put himself to sleep.

It was about the great battle between the beasts and the birds—the real reason why the owl was reduced to shame and forced to cover himself with night.

"And they came from the North and the South and the East and the West in flight, oh, many ri broad. The quails from the millet, the stork from the river, and from the pond the king-fisher, flashing like a blue jewel in the sunlight.

"Then said the stork, who led all these people of the air:

"'Behold! we are all assembled but where tarries Sir Owl?'"

"Then a sparrow made answer and said:

"'As I paused to rest on a cherry bough, for my wings be little though my heart is big, I heard Sir Owl in treasonable conversation with a rat. And said he, "Come forth from thy burrow, O Rat, that I may feast my eyes upon thee; and the empire of the beasts shall be thine, and also the empire of the birds."'"

"And the voice of the Hidden One replied—"

But what the Hidden One made answer, Leslie did not remember, for the artless story had lulled him to sleep.

CHAPTER XVIII

MOSTLY ABOUT FLOWERS

O Japan! Spring! Dawn! what an exquisite and roseate mystery surrounds the meeting of ye three!

Night, and the owls, and the ghosts, have vanished, day and the sparrows have come.

Up from Nagasaki rise the murmurs of life, mists are vanishing from the hills across the harbor, where the lateen sails of junks are rising to find the wind, and the sampans dart about like attenuated water-beetles.

The far, faint sound of a bugle from the man-of-war anchorage crosses the far, shrill crowing of a cock owned by Mr. Pinecape, the cobbler of Jinriksha Street—two rapiers of sound crossing each other in the now brilliant air. Then the noises of the day deepen, and the whirr of the cicala mixes with all sorts of faint domestic noises, a *mèlange* from which the ear can pick out notes just as the eye points in an impressionist's picture: the clatter of a pair of clogs, the call of a watercress seller, the clash of a tin pan dropped somewhere, and then cock-crow after cock-crow from far and near, some loud and defiant, others defiant enough but faint, as if coming through a pin-pole half a mile away.

The kitchen of the House of the Clouds is a square apartment, with no matting on the floor, and just now flooded with sunshine.

Leslie, in the early days, had caused to be constructed by a stranded ship's carpenter, a solid English kitchen-table of white pine. He wanted to give the man a job, and he thought the thing would prove useful; and it did.

To begin with, it smelt deliciously, and Mother Fir-cone amidst her avocations would take a sniff at it now and then, just as a snufftaker takes a pinch of snuff; she would also sit under it preparing sweet potatoes, stringing beans or what not; but as for using it as a table, such an idea never occurred to her. In fact, she had no ideas at all about a table, and was quite convinced that this gift of Leslie San's was a sort of pine-wood temple, constructed for the purpose of being sat under.

It was also a place of refuge in time of earthquakes, when the whole household, saving Leslie and Campanula, got under it for fear of the roof falling. It received the title of "Honorable," and was altogether a thing very much respected, and even vaguely beloved.

Under it this morning sat Lotus-bud, preparing fish for breakfast; on it (these new Mousmès used it as a shelf) reposed various paper boxes containing eggs and groceries, weird-looking boxes suggesting that a conjurer was about to commence operations, not a cook.

The sun laid a great square of light like a burning mat upon the floor near the table, and on her knees in the center of this mat of light sat Pine-breeze cleaning an hibachi. Cherry-blossom, the third Mousmè, squatted right before Pine-breeze doing nothing.

From under the table was escaping a faint blue haze of smoke. Lotus-bud had just taken a few whiffs from a tiny pipe.

They all smoked, these Mousmès, pinches of stuff like chopped hay in pipe bowls the size of a child's thimble; but Campanula had never acquired the art, though all her friends were ardent tobacco lovers. Leslie San had said "No," and that was enough.

As Pine-breeze cleaned the hibachi and made it spick and span, she was telling the others a yarn, mostly to do with her doings when down the town marketing last evening. How she had bought this or that, what had been said to her, and so forth—a tale simple enough, but a miracle of genius considering the tongue in which it was told. For in the Japanese there are but two parts of speech, the noun and the verb; these, and splinters and scraps of broken-up nouns and verbs, which, in the form of particles and suffixes, help to shore up the meaning and pin together the common sense, have to do all the talking.

The learner of Japanese feels at first like a person condemned to eat gravy soup with chop-sticks. Oh, for even a pronoun! Imagine talking to a person without being able to use the word "You," without being able to use the word "I"! Imagine the horrible tortures of a Japanese egoist on his death-bed making, or attempting to make, his dying speech!

But there are no egoists in Japan—can't be with such a language—and there are no purse-proud snobs, or if there are, they hide themselves very closely.

For self-depreciation is the key-note of Japanese conversation and manners.

So she goes on with her story, in a voice sweet to listen to as the ripple of a mountain brook, and Lotus-bud listens under the table, fish-knife held in air, for the tale is reaching an interesting point.

Then Campanula's voice is heard speaking to Sweetbriar San. She is coming to the kitchen to superintend things and—crack! the fish's head is cut off, and three Mousmès are working like one.

Campanula San is younger than any of these Mousmès, and she treats them like sisters, yet strangely enough, they do not encroach, but treat her as their mistress—a condition of things impossible in Europe, and presently, perhaps, impossible in Japan.

The sun has leapt now over the hills, and Leslie is heard moving upstairs. Pine-breeze claps her hands with horror, and rises to her feet: she has forgotten to fill his bath.

She goes to do so, and Campanula wanders out the front way to the balcony, where she pauses to gaze at the azaleas, shading her eyes with her hand.

The fire is spreading; another crimson blossom is almost unfolded, and others are soon to be born. Every spring the coming of the azaleas is an event in Campanula's life.

A wealth of crimson azaleas is one of her first recollections. Away beyond that crimson fire of flowers lies the land of her earliest childhood. The house with the plum tree, very vague indeed; the father who hit things with a hammer, still vaguer; the sugar-candy dragon lost, and so miraculously recovered; the little boy who went to sleep in the snow—or was it in a field of lilies?

Her real life, it seemed to her, began as she was reaching for a crimson blossom one day in a field of crimson blossoms, and was suddenly caught up sky-high by a thing taller than a tree, who did something to the side of her neck, just under her left ear, that was not hurtful or particularly unpleasant, but which, nevertheless, made her scream.

Then, behold, she saw that the thing was a man, though in strange clothes, but he did not frighten her in the least, and she gave him her hand at once, and with confidence, whereupon he took her in his arms and carried her to a road where stood another man, all black, even to his hands, but his face was white, and he had a red beard.

Then this man, who was also unfrightful, began to make her remember things that she had for the moment forgotten. To remember her father, and the fact that she had lost her way, and other things too, including the errant dragon. He made her remember that she wished to get back to her father, but she did not remember this so very clearly. In fact she was quite content to go with these two men over the hills and far away, feeling sure she was safe with them, went they where they would.

The scenes on the road to Nikko she remembered: a funny man away in the distance dancing amongst trees, and the entry into Nikko borne sky-high above all the other children, the Tea House of the Tortoise, and—grandest remembrance of all!—the miraculous awakening with the long-lost dragon in her hand. He was so full of mystery that she never had even dreamt of eating him, and she still possessed him. He was upstairs in the drawer of a lacquered cabinet, cracked, it is true, by changes of temperature and warped in the back, for age touched all things, even sugar-candy dragons.

Then there was her life at the House of the Clouds, the mission school; rainy days when she splashed through the mud under a broad paper umbrella; fine days when she flew kites with M'Gourley San, played hop-scotch with Kiku San and Kitsune Ken, with all sorts of other Sans, mostly with shaved heads.

This was Campanula's childhood as she remembered it. But as you cannot remember your childhood till you have stepped over the line where the child becomes a boy or girl, Campanula had not begun remembering it till about six months ago.

 Up till then M'Gourley San, and Leslie San, and Sweetbriar San, and a host of other honorable people surrounded her, one as important as the other, Mac perhaps more important than any.

Then all at once—in a week or so, to be more precise—a host of new ideas came to her, bothersome, formless ideas, as ungraspable yet as insistent as the great Boyg himself.

Then the ideas began to take form. It was in the garden one day. Her eyes fell on one of the flowerless azalea bushes, and she remembered how it had been covered with crimson flowers last year, and how beautiful they were, beautiful above every other flower, even the lordly peony, who seems to hold the whole glory and mystery of summer in the gloom of his splendid heart. And her mind wandered back from spring to spring, led by the crimson blossoms, till she called to mind the valley where Leslie had found her.

It was he who had found her wandering alone there, and he had picked her up.

She had never forgotten the valley; it had lain in the distance in her mind, but she had no use for it till now. Now it came to her in all its splendor, and explained to her why the azalea was the flower she loved above the peony, the lotus, or even that glorious mystery, the dragon-spume chrysanthemum.

Flowers are so bound up with the lives of the children of Japan that they have a meaning and speak a language to them almost unknown to us.

So Campanula sat immersed in her dream, and Leslie, who had swung a hammock between two cherry trees and was lying in it, little knew what was going on in the small head of the person seated near him on the square of matting. She had been doing some needlework, but her work had dropped in her lap, her hands were folded, and her eyes were fixed on the azalea bush.

Next day, or perhaps the day after, for a man's perceptions in these matters are sometimes dull, he noticed a change in her. He could not say what it was, but the submissive and humble person, the very fact of whose existence was a theme for perpetual self-excuse, had somehow changed. She was just as submissive and humble, but there was a subdued joyousness in her manner when excusing her existence as though she thought that somehow it might not be such a frightful crime after all, and perhaps capable of condonation some day.

Then, when he called for his cigar-case Pine-breeze did not appear with it, though Pine-breeze loved to be the carrier of it, because it was a foreign thing, and the leather smelt deliciously.

Campanula brought it *and* a match-box, a thing that Pine-breeze's flighty little mind nearly always forgot.

A few days before, Leslie had possessed three servants and what he called an adoptive daughter. Then he suddenly found himself in the possession of four servants, one of them more attentive than the other three put together. He put it down to the fact that her housewifely instincts were awakening, and as the change in her wrought for his comfort and ease he did not speculate on the cause as he would have done had the reverse been the case.

Women are curious creatures, as the philosophic Mac once said. But on the whole, in their way, I think men are just as strange.

Kite-flying had now been put aside with other childish things, and the tiny hands that had grasped the sugar-candy dragon were now preparing to grasp the real business of life: a business whose main objective was the happiness and comfort of "He who is taller than the tallest of trees."

Pine-breeze, Lotus-bud, and Cherry-blossom. Looking at them in a row, you might have thought them pretty much alike, as far as mind and spirit were concerned, just as three sleek, well-groomed ponies may seem identical— until you try to drive them.

It was not till Campanula took the reins that she found the three underlings were each afflicted with a special infirmity, or rather special infirmities.

Pine-breeze was such a scatterbrain that if you sent her down town in a hurry for eggs she would, as likely as not, dawdle home in an hour with tomatoes and some wild tale picked up on the way, pleasant and interesting enough, no doubt, but useless for the purpose of making an omelette. She would leave Leslie's bath unprepared, and then, sitting in her own tub, would clap her hands with horror at the remembrance of her own forgetfulness, and as likely as not attempt to rectify her error attired in a bath towel; and she would smash things—crockery ware understood—with almost the facility of your Western parlor-maid. To make up for these bad points, she was literary above her class; had a passion for flowers above her fellows, and had composed a poem about a grasshopper.

Lotus-bud was the cook; her infirmity was weakness. She would sit and listen to Pine-breeze's idle chatter and let the bread burn. Pine-breeze could work and talk, but Lotus-bud could not even work and listen. So she would sit with her hands in her lap, listening. She made a splendid audience but a somewhat indifferent cook.

As for Cherry-blossom, she was purely and simply an idler, a lotus-eater, a hobboe in the guise of a butterfly. A thing so fragile and pretty, so perfectly dressed and so seemingly boneless, that you felt to expect work from her would be absurd; which, indeed, it would have been.

For she never worked, she dreamed.

She was enamored of a riksha man, and she would go out and meet him under the lilacs at the gate, and then vanish with him to goodness knows where for the evening.

He was the strangest natural phenomenon, this lover of Cherry-blossom's, for he was always changing in size, and his face was never scarcely twice alike, and his number—rikshas are numbered just like hansom cabs—was

255.66.7.103.and 42.

At least Pine-breeze, who was an observant body, got that far in her notation, and then gave it up as a bad job.

All these things, and more, Campanula had to cope with, and she did so with more or less success, gaining in her experience much that a girl of her age is supposed not to know, but losing nothing either in gentleness or modesty.

She brought Pine-breeze to a vague sense of the wrongfulness of flighty ways, and with her own little hands she made new bread to replace a batch of loaves burnt to cinders by Lotus-bud (bread that gave Leslie indigestion for a week).

As for Cherry-blossom, she told her, missionary fashion, that she would certainly go to hell and be burnt like Lotus-bud's loaves if she did not stop vanishing down town with riksha men; and Cherry-blossom ground her nose on the matting and wept, and promised reformation, and went out two nights afterwards with No. 173 to a grand blaze up at the O Suwa temple, where she devoured candied beans and comfits, and bowed before graven images, and had a general good time with a host of "heathen" people like herself.

Cherry-blossom's rikshas never cost her anything. Love lent them to her.

Leslie's socks up to this had always been vanishing, and the ones that remained, were always, or generally, in holes. The Mousmès said it must be the mice. Campanula, however, found Pine-breeze one morning cleaning a kettle with a silk dress-sock. It seemed silk socks at half a guinea a pair gave a polish nothing else would give.

The kettles were duller after that, but the depredations of the mice ceased.

Having looked at the promise of the azaleas, she went in to see how things were getting on.

Presently she and Leslie were seated at breakfast opposite to one another on the floor. Leslie, attired in a suit of faultlessly fitting pale gray tweed, looked much more like an Indian cavalry officer on leave than an umbrella merchant, as he called himself. He had arranged to call for Jane du Telle at ten o'clock to take her out shopping; the gloomy thoughts of the night before, the effect of the opium, and the effect of the dream, had vanished.

He was sipping his tea, and glancing over the *Japan Mail*, when Campanula interrupted him.

"What iss Dick?" she suddenly asked; she prolonged her s's in the faintest degree, difficult to reproduce in print, for there is no type capable of representing an s and a quarter.

"What is what?" asked Leslie, lowering the *Japan Mail*, and staring at his pretty *vis-à-vis*.

"Dick—she called you Dick."

"Who?"

"She who gave you the flower," said Campanula, lowering ever so little her head.

"Which flower?"

"The one in your coat—yesterday."

"Oh," said Leslie, remembering a bluebell that Jane had plucked and given him as they went down hill the day before, and remembering also that George du Telle and Campanula had been walking behind and must have seen the transaction. "She calls me Dick because that is short for my name."

"Dick," murmured she, in a meditative voice.

She seemed turning the name over in her mind. Tasting it mentally, so to speak.

"She is an old friend of mine," continued Leslie. "I knew her, Campanula, before you were born, away over in another part of the world, where half the year it snows and where the wind blows just as hard as it does in Nippon, but the wind never brings flowers as it does here."

"No flowers," she murmured, incapable of imagining such a land.

"Only flowers like that blue one, and wild roses and a few others, but you never see camellia trees growing by the roads, nor lotus flowers on the ponds."

"Nor azaleas?"

"Nor azaleas—at least, as they grow here."

A shadow crossed the open doorway.

"M'Gourley San," said Campanula, who was seated facing the door.

"Dinna rise," said M'Gourley. "I've had ma breakfast, and I'll juist tak a seat on the verandy till y've done."

"I'm done," said Leslie, forgetful of grammar, and rising up, he came out, the *Japan Mail* under his arm, and a briar root in his hand.

They talked business a while, and then Leslie said:

"I say."

"Weel?"

"You remember that woman I told you of on the Nikko road?"

"Which wumman?" asked Mac, taking up a pebble from the path just by the veranda, and shying it at one of the hills of the landscape garden.

"Girl, I meant; you remember the girl I told you of?"

"Oh ay; the lass that flung you ower board—what of her?"

"She's here with her husband."

"Whaur?" said Mac, turning his head as though he fancied Jane and her spouse were camping out in the garden.

"She's staying at the Nagasaki Hotel with her husband."

"Whoat's their names?"

"Du Telle."

Mac doubled himself up for a moment, alleging for reason a touch of the stomach-ache, as a matter of fact it was a touch of internal laughter.

The day before yesterday he had found the newly-arrived George du Telle in the smoke-room of the Nagasaki Hotel, stood him drinks, and conducted him to Danjuro.

There they had saki and pipes, and George du Telle had bought a Pickford's van-full of rubbish, and parted with a fat green check on Cox's. An exceedingly fat check written with one eye shut, it is true, but quite in order.

"I dined with them."

"Ye whoat!" cried Mac, coming back from a vision of the victorious Danjuro doing the cake-walk amidst his bronzes and lacquers, kimono pinched up on either side between finger and thumb, his nose in the air, and on his face an assumption of stiff and haughty pride enough to kill one with laughter.

"Weel! weel!" said Mac, addressing the hills of the landscape garden.

"What are you weel-weeling about?" asked Leslie irritably.

"I am not a puncteelious man," said Mac, still addressing the hills, "in the small concairns of life, but if a lassie had treated me same's she you, *I'd a seen her dammit before I'd ha' dined wi' her.*" He shouted the last words, and brought his big fist down on his knee with a bang.

"Don't shout," said Leslie, "and make an ass of yourself. We didn't quarrel when we parted; we parted good friends. She didn't want to marry me—well, that was her look-out."

"I wish they hadna' come," said Mac gloomily.

"What on earth is the matter with you *now?*"

"I've seen the waurld," said the Gloomy One, "and I've seen wummen. And I've seen *her*—saw her in the smoke-room—" He stopped.

"What smoke-room?"

"Of the hotel. I was havin' a crack wi' her husband day-fore yesterday, and in she come to speak a word to him; and I know wummen—and, weel, I know, fixed between that chap with a head like a blazin' whin-bush and you, which way she'll run."

"I wish you wouldn't be such a fool," said Leslie, now really annoyed and therefore keeping himself in check; "she's nothing to me."

Mac turned, and under his bushy, half-grizzled eyebrows stared in Leslie's face, and Leslie did not support his gaze, but turned away irritably, and flung stones at a brown hawk that was circling in the air before them.

Mac got up, tapped the ashes out of his pipe, and made off.

"See ye the morn?" he called back as he got to the gate.

"Maybe," said Leslie, looking at his watch and rising to go into the house.

He went down at ten, and shortly after his departure, out came Campanula, a basket in her hand and sandals on her feet, for the weather was dry. She came along the path towards the cherry trees, examining the ground and the interstices of the bushes.

At last she saw what she wanted, a bluebell.

She plucked it with tender care and put it in her basket, then she saw another and treated it the same, and another; so went she on till it became perfectly plain that her object was not gardening, or the gathering of a bunch of flowers, but the extermination of every bluebell on the premises.

When the place had been cleared and the basket was half full of victims, the question came how to dispose of them. Impossible to throw them away or burn them; she would as soon, almost, have treated children so.

She stood at the gate undecided, till suddenly there came the solution of the problem, and opening the gate she passed down the lilac-shaded path to Nagasaki. On the way she saw more bluebells and stopped to pluck them, so that when the lane at the bottom was reached the basket was nearly full.

In a rabbit-hutch of a house off the lane lay a tragedy, or the remains of one, in the form of O Toku San, a poor work-girl. She had loved a man, and he had not even betrayed her in the ordinary way. He had simply changed his mind, and gone off with another girl.

She tried to kill herself, not in the native way, but with some abominable sort of foreign poison—Oxalic acid, most likely; but they saved her life, and she lay in the hospital nearly a month with her hands tied, to prevent her trying to kill herself again.

When she came out of the hospital she made no more attempts to obtain peace. She was in the clutches of pernicious anæmia, and she now lay dying, a despairing shadow, the ghost of what had once been a pretty and happy girl.

Campanula turned to the tiny house, and that day O Toku San had a whole silver yen to give to her mother on her return, and a bunch of freshly-gathered blue flowers to charm her eye: things to the dying better than all music and poetry, and far above the greatest masterpieces of art.

CHAPTER XIX

THE STORK AND THE TORTOISE

They were in the street running parallel with Jinrikisha Street, a street truly of the old time, narrow with the house-tops, when the houses had upper stories over-leaning the way.

Jane seemed fascinated by the contents of the little shops, that sold everything from cuttle-fish to paper lanterns. Shops that were, most of them, simply raised platforms, matted and roofed.

Here abounded the tortoise-shell carvers, and the men who can make a netsukè to charm the eye out of anything: a knot of wood, a shark's tooth, a useless bit of ivory.

"I'm going to buy things," said Jane, looking with a lustful eye on the cheap, or seemingly cheap, curios exposed for sale in some of the shops: old bronze gongs, kettles, sword guards, broken crockery were carefully mended, lamps, such as the Chinese magician might have hawked at the back entrance of the palace of Aladdin, fans, trick toys, and tiny boxes for holding rouge; tobacco-monos and opium pipes, broken-down English umbrellas, lacquer trays, and a heap of other dust-traps utterly useless, and some of them not very ornamental.

"If you *will* waste your money," said Leslie, "I'd advise you to come to Danjuro's. We can get to it by this lane, and I won't let him swindle you beyond the ordinary tourist pitch."

"Very well," said Jane, turning from a booth bearing this cabalistic inscription on its front, "Come rightin!"[2] "The things look pretty dusty, and I don't see anything I very much want—I'd like to buy *that*, though." She pointed to a mite in the colored kimono, playing battledore and shuttlecock in the gutter with another mite of its own size. "They seem so happy and jolly, these Japanese children, and clean, and I read somewhere they never give any trouble, or break things, or annoy people—Bless the child!"

[Footnote 2: I presume "Come right in!" was the artist's intention.]

A shuttlecock hit her a slap in the face, and the shuttlecock hitter laughed, and trotted after it, without any semblance of apology to his target.

"There's another illusion shattered," said Jane, wiping her face with her handkerchief.

"Have you—" began Leslie.

"What?"

"Any children?"

"No," said Jane; "I have not."

The stork on the tortoise, emblem of eternal life, and a "supposed" masterpiece of the great Miochin family of metal-workers, still stood on guard in the fore-front of Danjuro's wares. It was the same stork that Leslie had seen five years ago—at least, in appearance. In reality it had been sold five or six times during the last five years.

The selling of the thing always brought forth Danjuro's latent sense of humor, and could Danjuro the actor have seen his namesake at these supreme moments of trade, he would certainly have claimed him as a brother in art.

It would be an American woman, perhaps, in a blue veil, and with a smattering of knowledge picked up from artistic books about Japan. Mac would be the go-between, translating the desires of the female into Japanese for the edification of Dan, who spoke English, by the way, as well as Mac, and even, perhaps, better.

"Sell it!" Danjuro would cry. "I would as soon think of selling my own mother. Tell her Augustness to ask of me anything else. It is a piece of true Miochin, owned by my father, and his father before him. It has always brought my family luck, etc."

All of which M'Gourley would faithfully translate with the addition:

"He's the greatest auld scamp in the waurld; he's only puttin' up the price. Bide a wee, and let him simmer doon. It is not a true Miochin, but it's a vara excellent imitation, made, mayhap, by some pupil of the Miochins. Would y' be wullin' to pay twanty poonds?"

The Blue-veiled One assenting, Mac and Danjuro would go for each other in Japanese, and after five minutes' ferocious wrangling, and five minutes more of interpretations, the thing would change hands at twenty-five pounds, to be replaced next day, or, at least, the day after the departure of the Blue-veiled One from Nagasaki, by its twin image. A man at Osaka made them by the gross, and he charged two pounds ten a-piece for them to the trade.

Fortunately, the dead know not the doings of the living, else would the artistic Miochin family be turning eternally in their uneasy graves, with the rapidity of spinning bobbins.

Danjuro came out with his usual profound salute and low hiss.

Hiss is perhaps not the proper word, for the sound is made by the intake of air between closed teeth, and is intended to represent delight beyond words.

And, indeed, when Danjuro beheld M'Gourley entering with a client ready to be shorn, the sound came from him as no empty compliment, but as a natural expression of his true feelings.

It was different as regards Leslie. Danjuro looked on Leslie with the nervous dread with which you or I might look upon a mischievous lunatic.

Leslie had once nearly spoiled a bargain—a delightful bargain from the dealer's point of view, a disgraceful swindle viewed by the cold light of English ethics.

An English Member of Parliament had been trepanned into paying two hundred pounds for a pair of vases worth, maybe, twenty. Mac in his jubilation boasted before Leslie, and Leslie had "put the stopper on," caused the money to be returned, with a note to the effect that the jars were now discovered (from some documents connected with them) to be imitation, and not as represented when bought.

The Member of Parliament, instantly concluding that *this* was a swindle, and that he had obtained priceless articles by accident, refused to accept the money, or return the jars.

And thus was he done brown on his own spit, and basted by his own right hand, for in his book of travels, "Amongst the Japs," he mentioned the transaction, and, worse still, sent a copy of the book to Danjuro, with the passage marked with blue pencil.

Dan read the passage with the aid of a pair of horn-rimmed spectacles, and with a face mirthless as a shovel.

But the soul in him bubbled. He could quite understand the Member of Parliament's point of view, but Leslie's was quite beyond his power to grasp.

Honesty for the sake of honesty, and without any ulterior reason, even Art for Art's sake was more understandable than that.

So he hissed without pleasure as he bowed before Leslie and Jane, imploring them to condescend to make the honorable entrance, and intimating that everything in the place was theirs.

Jane nodded to him, and looked round.

"There's one of the monstrosities I told you of that George bought the other day," said she, pointing to a bronze frog half as big as an ordinary coal-box. "Oh, look at *that*!"

She pointed to a furious struggle in bronze between a man and a monster. The monster had opened its mouth to devour the man, and the man had caught it by the tongue, which he was tearing out.

It was the climax of the fight, and the conclusion one could read in the triumphant ferocity of the man's face—a thing to make one shudder.

"Danjuro San," said Leslie grimly, speaking in Japanese, whilst Jane gazed at the fighting group, "this is the lady whose husband you and M'Gourley San entertained the other day—the Red-headed One. She is a friend of mine, and I pray you to entertain her differently."

This is a vague interpretation of the Japanese for "This is the lady whose husband you swindled the other day, but if you play any of your tricks with *her*, I'll make you sit up—see?"

To fight with a Japanese you must come to blows, for you can't possibly do it in words properly. The old Japanese who made the language had no use for terms of abuse: swords were good enough for them.

"I'll have that," said Jane, suddenly seizing the fat baby, the size of a tangerine orange, done in ivory and engaged in feeding ivory ducks on top of a lacquer cabinet, "and the ducks. Tell him to send them to the hotel; you can fight with him about the price afterwards—and those two vases; and oh, that ivory Mousmè with the umbrella—isn't she sweet! I don't see anything else I want. *You* have something, I want to make you a present."

"I don't want anything, I'm tired of curios."

"Well, you'll just have to want something, for I'm going to make you a present. I'll give you this."

She took up a short sword in a carved ivory scabbard. On the ivory handle of it was figured a grimacing god, dancing apparently. She drew the blade, polished and razor-sharp, and then returned it to its sheath.

"Take it; it will come in handy when those robbers you told us of last night at dinner come again."

"I don't want the thing; it's unlucky to give knives."

"It's not a knife, it's a sword!"

"All right," said Leslie, "anything for peace;" and he took a great sheet of rice paper from Danjuro and wrapped the thing carefully up.

"Now," said Jane, "I want something for langn-yappe, as they say in New Orleans—something thrown in."

Danjuro declared that the whole shop was hers to do what she liked with.

"I don't want the whole shop," said Jane, "but I'll have that." She took possession of a tiny rose tree in the pot, a rose tree with blossoms the size of farthings.

"Now come."

"One moment," said Leslie.

His ear had caught a familiar sound. It came from the cellar where many of Danjuro's goods were stowed; it was the voice of Mac, and it came up like the voice of the Hidden One in Campanula's story. Mac evidently had a victim in the cellar. Leslie went to the cellar stairs and listened.

"I would not let him see you're wanting it. Juist assume a casual expreesion as if ye were na so vary carin' whether ye got it or no'. He'll be sure to tell ye it's a piece o' Miochin—it is *not*."

"How much do you think it's worth?" (A burly English voice, suggestive of shepherd's plaid trousers, a corporation, gold albert, and double chin.)

"All of fifty pounds, but not a penny more, not a penny more. Show him the money; there's not a Jap in Nagasaki can withstaund the sight of goud—or notes."

"Look here, if you get it for forty, I'll give you a ten per cent. commission."

"Am no so very carin' about commeesions; stull, as you offer it, I'll not say 'No.'"

The stork and tortoise were being sold again.

Leslie turned away in disgust.

"Come," he said to Jane, "let's go." And they passed out into the sunlit street, he carrying the parcel containing the sword, she the rose tree done up in rice paper pictured vaguely with the forms of storks.

"She has given him a wakizashi," murmured Danjuro, and he retired into a corner to smoke a whiff or two of hay-colored tobacco, and think inscrutable thoughts, before addressing himself to the victim that Mac was preparing down in the cellar.

"What shall we do now?" asked Jane when they were in the street.

Leslie thought for a moment.

"I'll tell you," said he. "We'll get rikshas and go to the cemetery—"

"I'll do no such thing," said Jane promptly.

"If you will allow me one moment—I'm not proposing to take you to a place like Kensal Green. A Japanese cemetery is worth seeing, just as much worth seeing as a Japanese town. Then we can go and have luncheon."

"Where?"

"Would you like to go to an eel-house?"

"Gracious, no! I hate eels. First a cemetery, and then an eel-house! I have half a mind to go back to the hotel."

"Well, a tea house, then; we can go to the Tea House of a Thousand Joys."

"Oh, that quite decides the matter," said she, assuming an outraged air, and hailing one of two rikshas that were passing.

Leslie hailed the other, and quietly directed the riksha boys to the cemetery.

CHAPTER XX

THE SONG OF THE MUSHI

"It almost makes one wish one were dead," sighed Jane. They were sitting on a moss-grown tussock near a grave adorned with a fresh spray of cherry-blossom, contained in a joint of bamboo. Beneath them the hill stretched downwards, terrace after terrace, casting before their eyes the cold color of marble, and the mournful green of cryptomeria trees, the delicate tracery of ferns, and the glory of the wild camellias. Beyond lay the blue of the harbor, black-blue where the wooded cliffs met the water; from the water the hills led the eye past camphor woods and the green of the young bamboo, up and away to where the brown of their summits cut the dazzling azure of the sky. "I have never seen anything so beautiful, so peaceful. What are you thinking of, Dick?"

"I was thinking," said Leslie, rousing himself, "that we might have luncheon at my place."

"You are perfectly disgusting!" said Jane. "I'll never go to a cemetery with you again. Luncheon! Who wants luncheon here?"

"Very few," said he grimly, gazing over the tombs.

"Now you're trying to be smart—at the expense of these poor things. Ah! look at that tiny grave with the white flower in the little vase."

"Some child."

"Yes; a thing with a great sash that was flying its kite or spinning its top the other day, and now it's here."

"Or hitting shuttlecocks about the street."

"Yes," wiping her cheek where the shuttlecock had hit her—then suddenly: "I think men are beasts," addressing the distant hills.

"I'm with you there."

"No, you're not; all men are just the same."

"I suppose you mean to infer in a roundabout way that I'm a beast. Thanks."

"There's nothing to be thankful for, only—they don't understand."

He took her hand in his as if to make friends, and she let him hold it for a moment, then she suddenly drew it away.

"Had not we better be going? What's the time?"

"Twelve."

"Will you come and have luncheon at the hotel?"

"No, thanks; why not come and lunch at my place? I'll give you all sorts of funny Japanese things to eat. Luncheon won't be till half-past one, but you can have a talk with Campanula. It will only take us ten minutes or so to get there from here."

They came down to where the rikshas were waiting; he helped her in, tucked the linen apron round her, and gave the men their direction.

Campanula San had not yet returned, declared Pine-breeze, as she kow-towed before them on the matting.

"Well, she won't be long," said Leslie. "Shall we go into the house or the garden?"

"The house," replied Jane. "I'm tired of the sunlight; let's go in, and sit on the floor and talk."

"Right. But do you mind—"

"What?"

"Well, as a matter of fact, there's a clause in the lease that no one is to go in with their boots on."

"Why, for goodness sake?"

"They say it spoils the matting."

"All right," said Jane, holding up a small foot, and trying to unbutton the shoe on it.

"Let me," said Leslie, going down on his knees.

The shoe came off, and the little foot in its bronze silk stocking lay in his hands for half a second—half a second during which he was seized with a wild desire to kiss it. Next moment it was out of his hands, and the other was presented to him.

"You are all thumbs!" said Jane. "Do be quick! I'm not a stork to stand on one leg for an hour. There, you've burst a button off! I knew you would. Stupid!"

"Pine-breeze will sew it on," said he, hunting for the button on his knees.

"No, she won't. It doesn't in the least matter. Gracious, Dick! when I see you just like that, crawling about on your knees—"

"What?"

"I can't help remembering—Do you remember the rainy day at Glenbruach, when you and I were playing marbles in the pistol gallery, and I said you cheated, and you said you didn't, and I said you did, and you called me a liar?"

"And you hacked my shins?"

"Yes; and old Mrs. Johnstone, the housekeeper, came in and saw me and said I was an 'awfu' lassie!' Can it be that all that really happened, and that we are the same people? Imagine me hacking your shins now! Imagine us both playing marbles on the veranda!"

"And we didn't speak to each other for a day," said he, following her into the house. "And you looked so stiff and sour, and all of a sudden you came up from behind and flung your arms round my neck."

"And you shouted: 'Oh, get away, you little brute!'"

"Yes; because I thought you were making another attack on me, and all the time you only wanted to k—"

"I didn't. I only wanted to apologize."

"Well, apologize, then!" said he, arranging the cushions on the floor, and placing the rose tree and the parcel containing the sword in a corner.

"It is sad to look so far away," said she, taking as comfortable a position as she could upon the cushions. "Life was so jolly then. Oh! a good old day's trout-fishing is worth all the money in the world. Money is no use; what's the good of it? It just makes one not care for the simple pleasures of life. Do you remember the picnic you and I and those American children, who were staying at Callander, had, when the soda-water bottle burst, and we found we'd left everything behind but the jam and the eggs? Dick, I—I—want to ask you something."

It was one of the peculiarities of Jane's mind that a question formulating there would work its way along like a worm, under, maybe, ten minutes of conversation, and then come out at the end of a paragraph, rise for air, so to speak, in a manner irrelevant and sometimes startling.

"Yes?"

"What became of you all those three years before you came here to Japan?—you vanished. You told me the other day you were in Australia; were you?"

"I was in prison."

She turned deathly pale, and stared at him as if he had struck her.

"Oh, you need not be so alarmed; it was not a criminal but a social prison. My father allowed me a hundred and fifty a year, paid quarterly, as long as I lived in Sydney, and as I had no trade and no money I lived in Sydney for three years—tied by the leg."

"I think you take a pleasure in frightening me; first you told me you were a shopman, now a prisoner. Dick, why do you *always* make your own case out worse than it really is? Tell me, what was the last quarrel with your father about?"

"Debts."

"And, Dick—you know you used to—"

"I know I used to drink, but I don't drink now."

They were silent for a while, then he began to speak and tell her the story of his life as a remittance man, and he did not spare black in the composition of his picture.

She listened at first interested and amused by the thought of Dick tied by the leg in Sydney, hobbled, so to speak, and made to behave.

Then her amusement gave way to compassion. She saw him wandering in the Domain, by the sea-shore, in the streets, a lonely figure, a man with no interest in life, an exile banned by society.

She thought of all the men she knew and the number of them who were just as wicked and foolish as Dick had ever been, yet who by keeping on the right side of their bank balance retained their social position and the respect of all men.

And thinking of all this the heart in her was moved. A most dangerous condition just now, for Jane, Bessemer steel in her everyday laughing mood, became wax when her compassion was aroused.

"Why didn't you write and tell me?" said she. "I'd have gone and seen your father. Oh, it was wicked to send you off like that, away from every one. *How* could a father treat his child so!"

They were silent again for a moment.

"Poor Dick!" said Jane suddenly, and she took his hand in both hers and stroked it. A little shiver went through him.

Then, all at once, she felt an arm around her waist and his breath upon her cheek, and she did not try to take her hand from his or struggle, nor, after the first second of troubled alarm, did she feel the wish to struggle.

She had ceased for the moment to be Jane du Telle, a married woman, a person with a stainless reputation. All these facts were swept away by nature, just as shrubs and fir trees are swept away by the rush of the avalanche.

A great faintness came over her. She clung to him, and sinking backwards, fell upon the matting; his arms were around her, his breath on her cheek, her lips were returning his kisses, yet all the time her lips were murmuring: "Don't—don't—don't!"

At this supreme moment came a sound strangely alien to the situation—the jingling of tea-cups no less—and through the wall, or at least the opening of a panel, entered Pine-breeze, followed by Cherry-blossom, with the luncheon.

"Dick!" she cried, sitting up with her cheeks raging red, "tell them to go away."

But Dick was not heeding her. He was sitting up with his hands to the side of his head, and an expression on his face that made her almost forget her own position before the Mousmès.

"Do you hear it?" said he.

"What?"

"That noise, my God, that noise."

A tiny cage was hanging from a hook on the wall. In it was a thing much beloved by Campanula—an insect like a grasshopper that sang a buzzing and tremulous sort of song. The mushi was a creature that only sang by night as a rule, but some spirit had moved its poetic soul, for it was singing now.

"It's that thing in the cage," said Jane, pointing to it tremulously, thankful for any excuse to escape the glances of the Mousmès.

He looked up, sprang to his feet, went to the cage, and tore it from its hook.

The Mousmès screamed out, for from his furious manner and the expression of his face they felt he was about to dash cage and mushi on the matting, and trample them underfoot.

And he was, for one horrible moment. Then something in him prevailed— the something that had made him pick the Lost One up and kiss her, and carry her all the way to Nikko; the spirit of good that had made him always not so bad as he might have been.

He rehung the little cage on the hook, and the thing in it became dumb; the sound in his head that troubled him had died away, and he returned to where Jane was sitting, and resumed his position on the cushions near her.

Then he told the Mousmès to leave what they had brought on the floor, and to go away till he called them.

"Oh," said Jane, when they were alone again, "to think they should have seen me like that. Oh, *Dick*! How could we—how could I—"

"*They* don't matter," said he gloomily.

"Oh, don't *talk* to me!" She wrung her hands.

"For goodness sake," said Leslie, "don't make mountains out of molehills. They saw me kiss you, well, what of that? and they don't talk English—at least, English that any one can understand."

"But like that on the floor," murmured Jane, comforted somewhat by the last statement.

"Well, what of that? We are in Japan, where people live on the floor. I admit if a servant in England came in and saw—"

"*Don't!*" screamed she; "don't speak about it again. It was a moment of weakness; let us forget forget it. I mean, let us *remember* it as a warning."

"Do you feel like eating luncheon?" he asked, looking at the pathetic little dishes and tea-cups, each on its sea-green mat.

"No; I feel like nothing. I only want to go and bury myself."

He poured her out some tea and took some himself.

"You frightened me," she said in a tremulous voice after they had sat for a moment in silence. "I thought you were going to do something dreadful."

"When?"

"When you took that cage down with the buzzing thing in it that annoyed you—poor atom!"

"It didn't annoy me; that was not the sound I heard. It was the sound I heard in the dream I told you of—that devil—"

A figure stood in the doorway: it was Campanula returned.

CHAPTER XXI

M'GOURLEY'S LOVE AFFAIR

Mac had gone down to the office that morning in a temper.

The staff consisted of himself and Ah Hop Sing, the Chinese office boy. He could not quarrel with himself, so he quarreled with Ah Hop Sing, using a rattan cane to enforce the argument, till Ah Hop Sing hopped and sang in a fashion that justified his title.

Then Mac wrote business letters and whilst he wrote, the thoughts of this dusty and unlovable-looking Scot went far astray on pleasant and picturesque roads, under blue skies, by brakes all gay with the crimson japonica flowers and the glorious beauty of the red camellias, and beneath the solemn darkness of the cryptomeria woods of Nikko.

That is to say, they would stray to these places, and then he would recall them to indite letters of advice to Maconochie of Glasgow, a letter of abuse to Mr. Oyama—a gentleman who never fulfilled his contracts when they threatened loss, sheltering his business self behind the ample kimono of the Tokyo guild—and letters to divers other people in trade.

And still his thoughts would stray whilst he gummed and stamped the envelopes, and they would be buying dolls now at booths in Jinrikisha Street, or helping to fly kites at the House of the Clouds.

They would stand watching a small person playing kitsune-ken with another person of her own age; and the same small person laboring up the Hill to the House of the Clouds, burdened with a bundle of books, and sheltered beneath a many-ribbed crimson umbrella.

Then they would glance at the same person, bigger grown, and suddenly become beautiful; then they would heave their shoulders and sigh, and all come back to help in the addressing of a letter to M'Clintock of Osaka, or some other magnate of the Jap Rubbish Trade.

Mac was in love, as I have before indicated: in love with three people. A tiny dot in a blue kimono and stiff sash; a person somewhat similarly dressed, whom he had sometimes helped of evenings with her lessons, or watched as she pricked her fingers over needlework; and a Mousmè as pretty as seven.

He had been in love for years without knowing it; a flower had been growing in this dusty soil, where one could not fancy any green thing finding nutriment, unless, perhaps, a weed. A white flower, pure and without stain.

Nothing could be more ideal than this love, nothing with legs and arms attached to it could be more un-ideal than Mac. And the strange thing was that this pure blossom of the soul did not improve the soul it grew from a bit, at least as far as human eye could see, for the man of the Great Tung Jade and the Lessar papers incidents was, morally, just the same—worse, if anything—as the wailing clients of Danjuro could testify.

When Campanula was alone with Leslie in these later days, she wore a grave and thoughtful air. Watching her, one could perceive that he alone possessed her mind; all the quaint and charming ways of her childhood, all things frivolous and light, she seemed to have dropped and left behind her with her toys.

When Campanula was quite alone with M'Gourley, a subtle change came over her. The child came out and played.

Though Leslie had adopted her as a daughter, she had by no means adopted him as a father.

Tod M'Gourley was her adoptive father, or, at least, she treated him as such. He acted also as uncle, aunt, grandmother, brother and general playmate all combined; and any half-holiday during the last few years, you might have seen Campanula and her family strolling along Jinrikisha Street, or on the Bund: the family in an old top hat, black broadcloth suit, and bearing a gamp umbrella in its hard fist.

They would stray together through the wonders of the town, Mac and she, and pause and gaze in at shops like two children, buy sweets and eat them unashamed and openly. Stop to look at performing monkeys, or listen to street ballad-singers, or criticize passing funerals.

He had never seen so much of life round town as Campanula showed him, clapping beside him in her little clogs when the streets were damp, or gliding beside him sandal-shod in the warm, dry days of spring.

Where Campanula was concerned, this dour and dusty Scot had all the delicate and instinctive feelings of a woman; he had noticed "fine" the change that had come over her of late, and the change in her manner towards Leslie.

The thing pleased him, yet it made him sigh—and frown, when he called to mind "that wumman," the mental label he had attached to Jane du Telle.

When he had finished business he went to Danjuro's shop, where he had an appointment, as we have seen, with an Englishman. The Englishman having been duly plundered, Mac looked at his watch, found it was nearly twelve, and was struck by a bright idea.

He would go to the House of the Clouds, fetch Campanula out, and have luncheon with her.

Ten minutes later found him on the veranda.

Campanula had just returned, having left O Toku San.

M'Gourley sat down on the veranda, and Campanula sat down beside him on a little fur rug made from the skin of an Ounce, or some such small animal. She looked sad and depressed, and her eyes wandered about the landscape garden as if questioning its hills, its streams, its old, old forests.

"Campanula," said Mac, taking her little hand between his great rough, red paws, "what ails you, child? You look sad and fashed, what's been worrying you?"

"I have been to see O Toku San," replied Campanula, speaking in Japanese. "She is dying. Her heart is dead," said Campanula, putting her other little hand over her own heart. "I am—oh, so sad! for to-day the thought of death has come to me, a thought that I never knew before."

"Child, child," said M'Gourley, "dinna speak like that. We must all die soon or later—ay, ay, we must all die, sure enough."

"But not so sadly as she," replied Campanula with a little sob.

M'Gourley looked at her; she was in tears.

He drew her close to him just as a mother might have done, and held her to him whilst she rested her head against his old coat, and sobbed and wept like a little child, gazing at the landscape garden through the veil of her tears.

He rocked her gently to soothe her, but said nothing, holding her just as he had held her that day in the gardens of Dai Nichi Do, as if to protect her against Death, as he had that day protected her against the vision of the terrible Akudogi.

Her sobs slowly ceased, but still she kept her cheek rested against his coat.

"What is Death?" she suddenly asked. The question was quite beyond M'Gourley.

"Dinna ask me," he said. "It's what we all must come to some day."

"And will O Toku San see him she loved when she goes—there?" continued she, as if unheeding his reply. "Perhaps"—after a long pause—"he will know her love for him when he too is there, and make her happy."

"Mayhap," said M'Gourley, who did not know the facts of the case, or perhaps he would not have taken so cheerful a view of O Toku San's lover's future state. "Mayhap." He looked down at her little face. Her eyes were dry, but a tear was still wet on her cheek. He took out his handkerchief and dried it.

Campanula smiled faintly, pressed her cheek ever so slightly against his arm as if in thanks, and drew away from him, resuming her position on the little rug.

M'Gourley took out his pipe, lit it, and began to smoke.

"Now," said he, "just put on those sandal shoes of yours again, for I am going to take you out with me."

"Where?" asked Campanula.

"No matter where," replied Mac, rising from the veranda. "A nice place where you and I'll go—you and I together, as we did along the Nikko road, only not on my shoulder. Na, na! you're ower big for that. Do you remember the sugar-candy dragon?"

"Ah! the Hon. Dragon!" replied she in the vernacular, as she bent to pass the sandal-strap past the great toe of her white tabi. "He is upstairs with—other things, but the Hon. Dragon is very old now."

Then she took her umbrella and opened it, and M'Gourley and she passed down the path to the gate.

He held the gate open for her, and she passed through with a murmured word of thanks, and then she led the way down hill under the perfumed beauty of the lilac boughs.

About half-way down, Campanula stepped aside as if to let some one pass. M'Gourley, close on her heels, and in a reverie, did the same thing unconsciously. If someone had passed, that someone must have effaced himself amidst the lilac trees on the left of the path.

"Poor blind man!" said Campanula, looking back up the path.

"Whoat?" cried Mac. "Whoat did y' say?"

"Blind man," replied Campanula; "he who came last night—you remember!"

M'Gourley took off his old top hat, and drew his coat sleeve across his forehead. Beads of sweat had sprung there all of a sudden.

He stood for a second or two looking at Campanula, and then for a second or two looking up the path, pied with sunshine and shadow, the pretty path that for him had suddenly been made horrible. There was nothing to be seen, nothing but the sunshine and shadow.

"My eyes are growing auld," he said at length. "Do you see him still, Campanula?"

She had turned away to look at a fern that was growing on the bank.

"I do not see him now," she replied. "He has gone through the gate."

"Are you sure," said Mac, speaking in a subdued voice, "that he was the same man that came last night?"

Campanula was quite sure.

"Wait for me," said Mac, "and I'll run up and tell them to give him some food."

He came hurriedly back up the path, very much against his will.

There was nobody in front of the house, he went round to the kitchen. The Mousmès were there, preparing luncheon—at least, preparing to prepare it in a leisurely way.

Had they seen anyone about the house, a blind man?

No, they had seen nobody, only the poulterer, who had been with eggs an hour ago.

Had they seen a blind man last night—had a blind man called round at the kitchen to ask for food?

No; nobody had been for food to the kitchen last night, least of all a blind man.

Then Mac hurried off, and the Mousmès dropped everything to discuss the meaning of all these questions asked by the Learned One; and Pine-breeze embarked on a story about two blind men and a frog, and the fox-faced representative of the rice god, a story that put the luncheon back half an hour.

Campanula was plucking flowers when Mac returned. Just three or four with a delicate fern frond, such a charming little bouquet, a veritable work of art made in a moment with unerring taste and a few turns of her deft fingers. She made Mac bend, and fixed the tiny bouquet in his coat-lapel.

Then they pursued their way, Mac vastly perturbed in his mind.

There was just now living in the pleasant city of Nagasaki an inn-keeper of the name of Yamagata, who owned a tea house named "The Full-blown Peony Flower."

Mr. Yamagata was a Progressive. He believed that a tea house where a real English luncheon or dinner could be obtained would, judging from his compatriots' passion for things European, be a success.

And it was, till half Jinrikisha Street nearly died of indigestion.

His tea house was a tiny affair situated up an entry near Danjuro's shop, and surrounded by a little courtyard, wherein grew dyspeptic-looking plum trees in pale amber-colored pots.

Danjuro, who was a friend of Yamagata's, had been chanting the praises of the place so long, that Mac had become obsessed by the idea of it; and casting about for somewhere new to take Campanula, the idea had turned up like a horrible sort of trump card.

The tea house was on its last legs, and practically deserted, so they had the place to themselves; and having ordered the meal they sat on the matting of a desolate room and waited for it to come.

"Campanula," said Mac, "you have never seen that blind man before?"

She shook her head.

"Never; nor one so ugly as he."

"Campanula," said Mac earnestly, "if you see him again dinna speak with him; he's an ill man and bodes no good."

Oh, indeed, she did not wish to speak with him, but he was so old and poor and ugly she could not but feel sorrow for him; and he said last night that he had come such a long way off, and must soon return.

M'Gourley shuddered.

"Ay," said he to himself, "a dom long way off;" then to Campanula: "Said he anything else?"

"No," replied Campanula, "for I told him to go to the back entrance, and he went."

At this moment the soup was brought in by three somewhat faded-looking Mousmès, each armed with a plate, a real English soup plate.

The soup was thin and not exuberantly hot, but it seemed vastly to amuse Campanula when it was put before her. "A," said she, pointing with her spoon-tip to something at the bottom of the plate, "B—C"—she was pointing to the little Italian paste letters floating, or rather sunk, in the mixture. "D—and look—a cow!"

Mac looked over to admire.

"Ay, ay, it's a coo, right enough, an' there's a cock and hen; but eat it up before it gets cold."

Campanula ate her alphabet, and the next course appeared. A boot sole labeled a beef-steak, which vanished, uneaten, and was replaced by what seemed to be an old stone cannon-ball, such as they used to fire out of Mons Meg. The O.S.C.B. was labeled a pudding.

It was the caricature of an ordinary English middle-class country luncheon.

But it was an amazingly clever caricature: a perfect work of art.

After luncheon, M'Gourley returned to business, and Campanula to the House of the Clouds.

CHAPTER XXII

THE COMPLETE GEOGRAPHER

On the way, she stopped at the shop of Mr. Initogo to pay a visit to her friend Kiku.

Campanula in her school-days had shown both qualities and defects of mind. At languages, at least in learning the English language, she was a success; a very moderate success where mathematics were concerned, though she knew enough to do long division, and to keep household accounts. They teach a lot of useful things at the mission schools—needlework, and so forth, and in some of these branches Campanula shone, but at geography she was a dismal failure. She had been always lacking in the power of location. Witness her first statements as to the whereabouts of the house with the plum tree in front of it.

The long sea voyage from Tokyo, or rather from Yokohama, had brought into her mind the impression that she had traveled to the end of things, yet they told her there were things beyond.

They showed her maps and globes. The maps were flat, and the globes were round, yet they said they were the same thing, or were pictures of the same thing. How a flat thing could be round or the converse, she could not say, but Howard San, the missionary, said they were. Was it for her to contradict him? So, instead of setting up her own wits against Howard San, and questioning him, she accepted his words just as you or I accept the words of mathematicians or physiologists concerning subjects on which we are ignorant. And thus on geography she got hopelessly muddled, and remained so.

This morning she was lamenting her want of geography, and casting about for some friend learned in the art. Of course she might have gone to Howard San, but she would have to wait till school was over, and, besides she felt a certain diffidence in approaching him on the subject, so she turned to the shop of Mr. Initogo.

Mr. Initogo was sitting on his heels on the floor of his shop, engaged in the gentle art of making tea; it was one of his fads that he always made his own tea with his own hands. Beside him stood an hibachi, on which a kettle was coming to the boil; before him, a tea-cup without a handle on a tray, and a microscopic tea-pot.

He warmed the tea-cup with a few drops of hot water; then, from a cylindrical tea-canister, with a thing like a snuff-scoop, he took a small quantity of green tea—tea of the color that an old black coat turns after years of sun and rain—this he popped into the tea-pot.

Then the honorable hot water being ready, he poured it into a porcelain dish to let it cool slightly, which it did, becoming converted during the act into the honorable old hot water.

The honorable old hot water being now ready, he poured it into the tea-pot, popped on the lid, looked up, and saw Campanula.

So immersed in his darling employment had he been, that he had not observed her entrance.

She wished to see Kiku? She was upstairs; this with a thousand apologies for his own blindness, and comparisons of himself with worms and other sightless things.

Campanula knew the way up; she had been up often enough before, and up she went.

Kiku San, since we hinted at her as a playmate of Campanula, had grown. The tumbling tot that Leslie had once caught by the "scruff" of her obi and held out at arm's length wriggling, for the amusement of M'Gourley, had become a Mousmè with a face at once heavy and flighty-looking; a broad face, pretty enough, but with a maddeningly irresponsible expression.

Pine-breeze was bad enough in the irresponsible line, but she could have learnt much from Kiku.

She was the dunce, or, rather, had been the dunce at the mission school; this is not saying very much against her, for Japanese girls are amazingly quick in the "uptake," learning coming to them as easily as ignorance to English girls; all the same she had been the dunce. She had never been able to conquer the letter "l" in English; and would say "raidy" for "lady;" yet she had a memory of sorts, blocks of facts swam in the ocean of her unintelligence like those houses that float about after an inundation of the Mississippi.

But the place left vacant in her skull by want of learning was by no means devoid of a tenant; therein dwelt a colossal impudence, a supreme self-assurance that sheltered and helped to hide the nakedness of her mind, and even obtained for her, amongst her girl friends, a sort of fungoid reputation for cleverness.

For when Kiku San said a thing, she said it with such assurance that it seemed true—the assurance of the absolutely untrustworthy intellect, which of all assurances is the greatest.

She was sitting now on her heels in a bare room on the upper floor, a tobacco-mono at her side, and in her hands a round flat box with a glass lid. She was playing at Pigs-in-Clover.

The two Mousmès bowed to one another with great ceremony, enquiring after each other's honorific health, and then Campanula came to rest upon the matting opposite to her friend.

They formed a pretty picture in the bare room with its chess-board matting, against the bare walls, whose only ornament was a kakemono representing Fuji San crested with snow.

Kiku was soon to be married—married to a government clerk to whom she had been engaged nearly since birth; and she entertained Campanula with long and uninteresting descriptions of her husband-to-be, his mother, his father, his grandfather, who lived at Nagoya, his brothers and sisters, how old they were and all about them.

Kiku was a bore, a female bore of the first water, and in this respect she could have given any old member of the Rag or Carlton points, and beaten him.

She told all these things looking up from under her thick eyelids, and with a half-smile, and Campanula listened, half mesmerized, wholly weary, but with all her courteous soul awake to do honor to the tale.

At last an hiatus occurred of which Campanula took advantage to ask the question in her mind.

Did Kiku, so learned on all subjects, know of any land where the snow lay for half the year?

Oh, certainly Kiku did, and she told about it.

Describing her future husband and his relations she had been vague and uninteresting, lacking, as she did, the gifts of perception and narration. But now, plunging into the empire of pure lies, she spoke with an assurance that made her words sound like gospel.

Such a country existed; as a matter of fact, she had it all in a book somewhere, but she did not need the book, as she never forgot anything. It lay in the sea beyond Nankin two hundred and sixty-seven ri beyond, and the snow lay there half a year, sometimes more.

"Is it a country where blue flowers grow, and roses—sometimes?" said Campanula.

"Just so, sometimes;" and Kiku, searching in the capacious bag of her ignorance, began to produce old broken-up facts that had been lying there like rubbish in the basket of a chiffonier.

The sea all round that place was frozen most of the year, and the sun shone once a month or so.

Then she painted a graphic picture of this desolate land which she declared to be divided into four parts, Unster, Munster, Rinster and Comit; and Campanula sat listening and receiving it all as truth.

Liars, somehow, are always sure of an audience; you and I, who speak the truth, the whole truth, and nothing but the truth, languish in conversation and are not heard, whilst your mendacity-monger holds the floor and absorbs the interest.

So Kiku San went on spinning her tale, and Campanula San sat opposite to her and listened, shivering at the dismal pictures being raised before her.

Then, all at once, from below came the irate voice of Mr. Initogo calling Kiku the "Heedless One." If he could have used a stronger expression he would have used it, for the dinner ought to be cooking at this moment, and the fish and seaweed had not arrived. The Heedless One had been, as a matter of fact, playing at Pigs-in-Clover all the morning instead of marketing.

The Complete Geographer rose to her feet in a hurry, for filial obedience resided in her breast, not so much as a virtue, but rather as a sort of mainspring put in by nature—or rather, I should say, heredity.

They went out together, and Kiku bought the fish and the seaweed and a few other important items, and then they parted, Kiku returned home laden with marketings, and Campanula to the House of the Clouds.

CHAPTER XXIII

THE STRUGGLE

Leslie walked back to the hotel that day with Jane. When he left her he was vastly troubled in his mind. Troubled about Jane, troubled about Campanula, troubled about himself, and troubled about a vast, vague, tragic something: a shadow stealing up from his past and already tingeing his future with the twilight that comes before eclipse.

What demon had called Jane up from the past?

Unconsciously during the last five years he had been altering for the better. The friendliness and kindness of Japan, the frank friendliness of M'Gourley, that most unconscionable Scot, the beauty of the flowers and seasons, and Campanula—above all, Campanula—these things had worked upon him with slow but sure effect.

Slowly, he had learnt the great, great secret that happiness is to be found, not in grand palaces, not in wealth, not in success, but amongst the lowly and little things of life, the things that no man can appreciate who has not a free and untroubled conscience.

The new book, the pipe of tobacco smoked beneath the cherry trees of a morning, the home-coming of Campanula from school of an evening laden with books and perplexities, the rubber of whist with Mr. Initogo, the quaint, funny things that are always happening in a Japanese household—these and a thousand other trifles had made up the sum of his life, and the addition of them made happiness.

And Campanula—he little knew how much she had entered into his being— what a multitude of impalpable threads bound her to him, threads that had been spinning from the very first day, when he found her lost amidst the crimson azaleas!

He had eaten the lotus for nearly five years; he had been preparing a future of happiness and peace, and who knows what boundless possibilities of love?

Suddenly, Satan had appeared before him with the command, "Get up and fight, fight me for this future you have been preparing for yourself; fight me for the beauty of it, the happiness you will have in it, the happiness you will make for others in it; get it if you can, for my weapon is Lust."

That night, when the moon, now waxing stronger, laid her patient square of pure white light on the floor of his room, the battle began in earnest.

He had determined on going to Arita on the morrow to get away for a while from the woman against whom he felt fate was driving him with ruinous intent.

Now, as he lay alone, with the powers of good and evil on either side of him, he reviewed his position clearly for the first time.

The cold, calculating, sneaking, pickpocket form of adultery, which is the canker at the heart of English society—to put it in plain English, the bestial use of another man's wife behind his back—was a form of crime as unthinkable to Leslie as the crime of cheating at cards, or forging a check.

To obtain the woman he wanted, there was only one way. The open way.

That meant the smashing up of everything around him. He must leave Japan, leave Campanula, for, deep in his heart, something told him that Campanula could have no place in that new life. It meant the social ruin of Jane du Telle.

Here, alone, away from the object of his passion, all this was very clear.

Then that same old Scotch ancester, with the long upper lip, and the crude common sense, and the rigid belief in God and the law, came out of his cell and spoke to this effect. There is no excuse before God or man for adultery. Love, the child of God, has no part therein, but Lust, the child of the devil, and the end of Lust is Hell.

All this, with the thoughts that went before it, was edifying and made for good, and the devil said nothing, for the devil, like the great Boyg, has a method with some natures. He does not strike, but lets the victim do the striking, hedging him gently, gently, letting him hit out widely till he is exhausted, or beats himself to death as the Blind One beat himself against the trees.

Early in the morning Leslie rose, white and haggard, and dressed, and went off to the station without waiting for breakfast.

"Tell Campanula San I am going to Arita on business, but will be back to-night. Tell her I am going alone," he said to Pine-breeze.

"Kashko marimashta," murmured Pine-breeze, in a voice of devotion, and he departed.

He was going to Arita to get beyond the reach of Jane, and lo! when he got into the railway carriage, she was there—not in the flesh, but in the spirit. And when he alighted at Arita, she was on the platform, and in the street she walked at his side.

The tones of her voice thrilled him, and he smelt the perfume of her hair, he felt the curve of her waist, and his lips felt the satin of her throat, but the physical desire was small compared with the terrible sentiment that was born of it, the heart-breaking longing inspired by her idealized image.

Passion, when it rises to this dimension in the mind of a man, has beautiful attributes as well as vile, it holds in its hands pictures of perfect innocence, besides the others.

The devil takes care of that!

He saw Jane not only as she was, but as she had been, fair, and fresh, and innocent, against the background of the beeches round Glenbruach, and the sea lochs, and the purple hills.

What he did with his body that day in Arita, or where he wandered, he could never tell, for his mind was fighting a battle so fierce that all intelligent perception of outward things was blurred.

At the end of it he found himself in a tea house sitting before some food which he had apparently ordered, and the battle was won. So he told himself.

As a matter of fact, he was worn out. Passion was exhausted, fighting against fate, attempting to escape from the pursuing devils, beating himself against the trees, he had fallen beneath them, telling himself that the battle was won, wondering at himself that he ever could have even dreamed of the ruinous course of action which lust had urged him to.

But the trees remained steadfast and unharmed, waiting only for the renewal of the madman's strength and the inevitable end.

It was dark when he reached the Nagasaki station. He picked a riksha from a row of them standing outside with hoods up, for it had been raining slightly, and looking absurdly like a row of tiny, unhorsed hansom cabs, and told the man to take him to the House of the Clouds.

He came up the hill-path, and as he came the wind, blowing against him, brought a perfume with it, the perfume of rain-wet azaleas. During the day and the previous night dozens of blossoms had broken forth, filling the garden with their fragrance and beauty; dozens more would be born ere the morrow under the light of the silvery moon now gliding up over the hill-tops behind a tracery of flying, fleecy clouds.

As he approached the house, he saw through the open panel space the silhouettes of Pine-breeze and Cherry-blossom.

They were sitting opposite to each other on their heels upon the lamplit matting, and seemed at first to be engaged in the game of kitsune-ken, but almost instantly he perceived that they were playing at no game, but were engaged in conversation. Alarmed conversation, to judge by the movements of their hands, now up-flung, now flung out sideways. Sweetbriar San was promenading the matting with tail fluffed out, now rubbing against Pine-breeze, now against Cherry-blossom, attempting apparently to join in the conversation, and seeming to share in the excitement.

Something had happened of a tragic nature—but what? Two steps brought him on to the veranda two more into the house with his boots on, despite the clause in the lease.

The Mousmès gave two little shrieks, wheeled round, and kow-towed before the August One.

"What is the matter?" he asked. "Has anything happened? Is Campanula San safe?"

Campanula San was quite safe.

Then why all this? What had they been conversing about with so many exclamations?

Confused replies.

"Go," he said, "and bring me some tea, and ask Lotus-bud to come hither."

In a few moments Lotus-bud, wearing a very white face, appeared, and kow-towed.

He questioned her. At first her answers were vague, and then it all came out.

Things had happened. Campanula San had gone into the town that day, and had met he whose head was like the rising sun (George du Telle in plain prose); and he with the sun-bright head had walked with her, and had spoken dishonorable words. Oh, shame!—he had offered her gold.

"God!" said Leslie, staring at the bent figure on the matting before him.

He remained speechless for a moment, then he took out his watch and looked at it: it was eleven o'clock.

He turned furiously and strode out of the room: on the veranda he stopped like a horse suddenly reined in.

Jane's image had appeared before him, turning him back.

Suppose he were to go to the hotel now and drag George du Telle out and beat him within an inch of his life, as was his intention a moment ago?

The idea of Jane in the midst of that scene brought his fury down from boiling point.

He returned to the room, where Lotus-bud was still on her knees, with her hands clasped.

Where was Campanula San now?

In bed and asleep. She had returned, it seems, greatly troubled at noon, and had confided her trouble to Lotus-bud, making her promise to tell no one— Leslie San especially—and Lotus-bud had promised—with the result we have already seen.

For a moment he thought of waking Campanula, but he dismissed the thought. The thing had occurred and was irremediable, the question now remained, what was he to do about George du Telle.

He went up to bed. In times past he could have obtained his remedy.

Where lay his remedy now? The law could do nothing; there remained only physical force.

A wheezy pug dog protected by a woman's skirts, that is what George du Telle was. Leslie knew that if once he could catch the brute by the scruff of the neck, the only struggle would be with himself as to the limits of chastisement to be inflicted.

If he could only get him away from Jane up a back street anywhere, just for five minutes! The thing was to be done. With the help of the astute M'Gourley he felt it was to be done, and would be done on the morrow.

He got up and went to a rack on the wall where he kept his sticks, and took down a whangee cane half an inch thick, a most efficient instrument for the chastisement of a brute. He made it sing through the air, then he put it on the rack again and returned to bed, and slept soundly, far more soundly than he had slept the night before.

CHAPTER XXIV

GEORGE DU TELLE

He was awakened by voices. Sunlight was streaming into the room, the sparrows were bickering round the trees, and from below came the voice of Pine-breeze crying, "Irashi, condescend to enter!"

Then Jane's voice: "I don't understand what you say. Stop rubbing the matting with your nose. I want your master." Then an octave higher, "Richard!"

"Hullo!" cried Leslie, leaning on his elbow, and scarcely able to credit his ears.

"Oh, you are there! Come down at once, I must speak to you. Quick!"

"What on earth has happened?"

"All sorts of things."

"I'll be down in two minutes, but for goodness sake tell me what *is* the matter."

"Can I speak without any one understanding?"

"Oh, that's all right."

"Well, then, George has bolted."

"George has *what*?"

"Gone away."

"Where has he gone to?"

"Oh! come down and I'll tell you everything. Dick! Dick! is that a bath I hear you dragging over the floor? Dick, if you dare to have the impudence to keep me waiting whilst you take a bath, I'll—I'll come up and pull you out of it. Do come on!"

"Directly!"

"Well, don't be long," grumbled Jane; and she apparently took her seat on the cushions upon the matting, for he could hear her grumbling about the absence of chairs.

This was a new development of affairs. George bolted! It was just what one might have expected of the man, to insult a girl and then fly from the wrath to come.

It was rather a relief, too, viewed by the light of morning. No man likes the task of thrashing a dog that has misbehaved: the thing has to be done, but it is unpleasant, and if the creature runs away and hides, so much the better. And the thrashing of a fat, wheezy pug without teeth or means of defense was what the punishment of George du Telle would amount to.

He dressed rapidly and came down to the room where Jane was sitting on a cushion, trying to read the *Japan Mail*.

"Oh, there you are! Come and sit down. No, not beside me; right opposite, if you please."

"Tell me all about it."

"Oh, there's not much to tell. I was in bed nearly all yesterday with a headache, and George went off for a walk in the afternoon; said he was going to call on *you*. I told him you had gone to Nagoya."

"Arita."

"It's all the same—then he went out, I don't know where, and that is the last I've seen of him. At nine yesterday evening they brought me a note saying he had gone to Osaka, and to follow with our luggage."

Leslie whistled.

"What are you whistling about?"

"Osaka! Why, that's over three hundred miles away!"

"Where is it?"

"On the Inland Sea."

"Where's that?"

"Oh, it runs from here up to—well, practically to Osaka. At least, it doesn't exactly reach from here, you have to go through the Straits of Tsu-shima."

"Well, I don't care what Straits you have to go through; he's gone to Osaka on important business the note said. Now, what business can have taken him there. What do they do at Osaka?"

"Make all sorts of things, from machinery to tea-pots, and so on."

"Well, he can't have gone to buy machinery or tea-pots—what can it *mean*? He was so good, too, yesterday; brought me up some antipyrine, and wanted to fetch a doctor, and plumped up my pillows, and then went out and off to Osaka without a word, and how did he get there? He says follow by next boat to-morrow. I was going to ask the hotel people, but I didn't like to. I just told them I knew he was going, and I was going to follow him to-morrow."

"There's no railway to Osaka," said Leslie, "for this bit of Japan is an island. He must have gone by a Holt liner; one started last evening. The Canadian Pacific boats don't stop at Osaka, they go right on to Yokohama. I suppose he means for you to follow by the Messagerie boat that leaves to-morrow evening."

"I'll give him tea-pots," said Jane gloomily, "when I catch him! The idea of his leaving me like that! In a strange country, too. I wonder *what* is the meaning of it all!"

"Perhaps he went away—because of a girl."

"You mean he's run away with some girl!" flashed Jane. "Why don't you say so if you mean it?"

"Because I don't mean it. I said 'because of a girl,' not 'with a girl.'"

"Dick, you know something!"

"Yes, I do."

Jane turned pale, and he hated to see her like that, but he had suddenly made up his mind to tell her all.

"He met Campanula yesterday afternoon, and, not to put too fine a point upon it, insulted her."

"Oh, Dick!" said Jane, turning, if possible, paler than before. She stared at him in a frightened way, then she recovered herself. "There must be some mistake; she must have misunderstood him. He couldn't have done such a thing; however foolish he may be, he's a gentleman."

"Yes, a gentleman in England, but not a gentleman in Japan. He—God damn it!" blazed out Leslie suddenly, bringing his fist down with a bang on the matting—"he offered her money."

"I must go to him at once," said Jane, making as if to rise, "and ask him if this thing is true."

"Sit down for a while; you can't possibly get to Osaka to-day. Oh, it's true enough. I was in a boiling rage last night when I came home and heard it all. I was going down to the hotel with a stick to have it out, and then I thought of you, and the disgrace and uproar there would be, so I just bit on the bullet and went to bed. Honestly, I was going to have got him somewhere by himself to-day, and have it out with him, but it seems he prefers insulting women to facing men. Forgive me, Jane, for all this; I feel bitter about it, but I hate to have to say these things to you."

"It was good of you to think of me last night," said Jane in a broken voice, gazing at the matting as she spoke, then looking up full in his face, "very good of you."

"Oh, I suppose it's really nothing, after all," he said. "Those confounded fools that write books about Japan have got it into English people's heads that every 'Jap-girl,' as they call them, is a what's-its-name at heart. Let's say no more on the matter, the affair is closed. Have some breakfast?"

"No, thanks; I'm too much troubled and worried," said Jane, sighing and folding her hands in her lap.

"Oh, don't trouble about it. I told you because—well, I thought you ought to know."

"Richard," said she, looking up, "if you meet George again—"

"Don't be a bit alarmed. I will do nothing to him except to cut him. He has run away; that closes the affair entirely. A man can only be really angry with a man."

"Richard," said she, now half tearfully, "I'm going to say something I want to say. Men don't understand women. I'm fond of George. Men are always talking about love, and so are novels. I never loved George that way. I don't think I ever loved any one really in that way, but I have an affection for George; I suppose that is the best name to give it. I know he's ugly, I know he's a lot of things he ought not to be, yet I feel he belongs to me.

"It's the sort of feeling one has for an—for an animal. I'm just telling you what I feel. An animal may be terribly ugly, yet one may love it. George has been very good to me, and he has grown into my life; that is the only way I can express it.

"Do you know, Dick, when you have your face very close to another person's face you cannot tell what they are like. Well, it's just the same with marriage. After people have been married some time they don't see each other as they saw each other before; they have lost their identity—each is part of the other. And, Dick, I know George has been wicked, but ought we not to remember, the day before yesterday—"

"Yes," he said; "the day before yesterday I kissed you."

"It was a moment of weakness on my part," continued Jane. "We are all very weak and wicked, but I have always been faithful to my husband—I should say, to myself. It is strange to talk like this."

"The whole affair is closed," he said. "Let us wipe the slate clean and begin again."

Sitting opposite to her here in the morning light he was a very different person from the man wandering about Arita yesterday, pursued by her image.

The course of a great passion like his is not a high level line. If a man were to live through such a phase of existence at Italian opera heights he would be mad or dead in a very few days.

Its course is most like the temperature chart of a typhoid fever case: tremendous ups and downs, fever point now, a few hours later almost normal.

He clapped his hands, and Pine-breeze appeared.

"Breakfast," he said. "You'll stay to breakfast," turning to Jane. "And there is something I forgot day before yesterday. You have come to see Japan—well, look here—"

He went to a big lacquer cabinet where he kept his papers, and returned with a large, square, cream-colored card covered with Chinese ideographs.

"What is it?" said Jane, turning it over.

"An invitation to a garden-party. A man named Kamamura is giving it to-morrow at O-Mura."

"A Japanese garden-party!" said Jane, with interest in her voice.

"Yes, very Japanese. He told me to bring any of my friends."

"But to-morrow," said Jane—"I am going away to-morrow."

The words went through him like a pang.

"Never mind," he said. "Your boat does not start till evening; you will have plenty of time to get back."

"I'd love to go," she said; "but—are you sure it's all right for me to go without an invitation?"

"Perfectly, or I would not bring you."

Pine-breeze entered with a tray.

"Where," enquired Leslie, "is Campanula San?" Campanula San had not risen yet; she had a headache.

CHAPTER XXV

RETROSPECTION

"I'll go up and see her," said Jane, when they had finished breakfast. "May I?"

"Yes, if you like; Pine-breeze will show you the way—but, Jane, say nothing to her of what occurred yesterday; she thinks nobody knows except one of the servants here."

"I'll say nothing," replied Jane; "but I've got some antikamnia tabloids in my pocket, fortunately, and I'll just make her take one."

"All right," said Leslie; "but for goodness sake don't poison her."

This was another point on which Jane had not altered. As a girl she had been possessed by a passion for drugs, and would swallow anything in the way of medicine she came across or was given. She had always been doctoring rabbits and other unfortunate animals, and had once nearly poisoned herself by taking half a bottle of pain-killer for a dose. And now here she was, nearly fifteen years after, in Japan, going upstairs to doctor Campanula, with just the same manner and seriousness of face with which long ago, medicine bottle in hand, she would give the order: "Prize its mouth open, Dick; don't hurt it. Steady now, I'm going to pour."

Quarter of an hour later she came down triumphant.

"She took it like a lamb. She's the dearest child! Now I'm off. I have a hundred things to do. Will you walk down with me as far as the hotel?"

He accompanied her to the hotel, and neither of them spoke much on the way.

"I won't ask you in," said Jane, when they reached the door, "because it wouldn't be proper. Now let me see. To-morrow is the garden-party; we might do something to-day, you and Campanula and I—might not we?"

"We could run over to Mogi," he said. "We can get rikshas, have luncheon there, and come back to tea at my place; and to-night there's an affair on at the O Suwa temple, we might go there. Shall I call for you at twelve or so?"

"Yes," said Jane, "if you'll bring a chaperon. You see, now George is away I must be awfully 'propindicular,' like that person in Uncle Remus—the Terrapin—wasn't it?"

"I'll bring Campanula—or one of the Mousmès, at a pinch."

"Campanula chaperoning me!" said Jane with a laugh. "Well, I don't care. It's only for the sake of Mrs. Grundy."

"There is no Japanese Mrs. Grundy."

"No, but there is an English one."

They parted, and Jane entered the hotel.

She went to her bedroom, got her writing-case out of a portmanteau, and began to write. She was writing a letter to George.

The first began:

> "Your abominable conduct has been discovered. You have heaped shame on me, you have heaped shame on yourself—"

When she got as far as this she found that it was too melodramatic, somehow, and the "heaped shames" did not ring true, so she tore it up and began again:

> "My cousin, Richard Leslie, sent for me this morning in great distress. *How* you could have acted as you did towards that sweet child surpasses me. Fortunately for yourself you have run away—"

She tore this up too, flew into a temper with herself, and then wrote as follows:

> "GEORGE,—I've heard everything. Dick is furious, but he's not going to do anything, so just stay at Osaka till I come, and don't go bolting off anywhere else. And don't drink too much port, for if you get another attack of gout *I* won't nurse you.—JANE.

> "*P.S.*—You ought to be ashamed of yourself."

She sealed this classical epistle and addressed it. Then she remembered that she might just as well have left it unwritten, for there was no communication to be had with Osaka till the morrow; and if she posted it, it would go by the same boat as herself. So she tore it up.

Then she sat down on the side of her bed and bit a corner of her handkerchief.

She was thinking.

To-morrow she would never see Dick again, most probably, after that.

She had never loved Dick, that is to say in the good old *Family Herald* way. Their boy and girl relationship had been anything but sentimental.

Recalling the past she could conjure up no tender pictures.

She could see herself clinging to a rod bent like a bow, and shouting to Dick: "Now then, chucklehead, gaff him!"

She could see herself tramping after him like a squaw after a chief on rabbiting expeditions—dozens of pictures like this, but none of them sentimental. She had never thought of marriage till the day she received a letter from Dick, asking her to marry him; to which she replied by writing half a dozen letters refusing him, which letters she tore up one after the other, and then wrote a seventh accepting him, which she posted.

Now one of the worst evils in an accepted proposal of marriage is this. That directly they hear of it, the girl's relations, male and female, take their implements—nets, ferrets, and so on—and go off rabbiting in your past.

Dick had not much of a past as far as size goes, but it was well stocked with game for hunters such as these.

So well stocked that old Mr. Deering, a retired London wine merchant who had taken a country seat in Scotland, near Glenbruach, put his foot down and forbade Jane to have anything more to do with her cousin: an order which would have driven her straight into his arms, had not the unfortunate Dick, hearing of the inquisition that had been made, come North inflamed with rage and whisky.

Men drank harder even in the 'eighties than they do now, and Scotland was never the home of abstinence; yet the scene Dick Leslie created in Callander went beyond the bounds of even Scottish convention, and utterly destroyed any chance of his marriage with Jane du Telle.

Remembering his description of the affair which he gave to M'Gourley on the Nikko road, you will agree with me that he was not a man who viewed his own acts—well, as others viewed them.

In this, however, he was by no means singular.

Jane, sitting on her bed and biting the corner of her handkerchief, was at the same time looking back back over the past. She was a person with an infinite capacity for affection, with no capacity at all for a Grand Passion. Her life was made up of a bundle of petty interests, and her history was the history of a pure and somewhat commonplace soul.

She had loved Dick as a brother in the past, and now that he had come into her life again after all those years (even after that terrible scene long ago), bringing with him so much from the happy days that were for ever gone, her heart went out to him as it had never gone to human being before.

And to-morrow she must say good-bye to him, and never, perhaps, see him again.

They must part; there was no other thing to be done. She was her own mistress, with plenty of money at her command; she could have flown in the face of society, and made Dick forever her own. Such a course did not even occur to her, for she was a creature bound by the laws of convention, almost as rigidly as you or I by the laws of gravity.

Out of very light-heartedness she would do things and say things that would have been dangerous symptoms in a woman of a sterner mold; and men had often pursued her, led on by this laughing spirit that vanished behind a veil, which, being lifted, disclosed an adamant door.

Her great danger lay in her compassionate emotions, and all the womanly nature that lay behind them. Her great danger lay in Richard Leslie, for he was the only being that had ever aroused them to their full strength.

All at once she cast herself upon the bed, and after the fashion of her childhood, buried her face in a pillow, and sobbed, and "grat."

When she had occupied herself thus for some ten minutes, she rose and looked at herself in the glass, and wondered at her own distorted image, and how she could possibly be such a fool. But she felt better; the pain of parting with Dick was not quite so bad, and she felt kindlier towards George.

If his conduct had taken place in England, I doubt if her anger would have been so soon assuaged. But they were in Japan—and the Japs, you know!—

PART THREE
THE BROKEN LATH

CHAPTER XXVI

THE BROKEN LATH

A heat wave from the Pacific had stolen over Nagasaki, and the windless night was filled with stars and lights.

Stars in the sky, and stars in the harbor, long wavy reflections of light from the ships in the anchorage, and ten thousand lanterns spangling the mysterious city.

A spangle of colored lamps that spread away to the base of the O Suwa hill which they stormed, covering it with a thousand sparkles like phosphoric sea-spray, and cresting its summit with a burning zone, bright as the snow crest of Fuji.

It was a gala night, and the O Suwa, that galaxy of temples, had called the true believers in love and beauty to worship in the name of religion.

From the great double temple, which is the crowning glory of the hill, Leslie and his companions looked down upon shrine after shrine, broad flights of steps stained with the soft amber and pink of lantern light, and the colored crowd ever shifting, and murmurous as the sea.

The shadow spaces and the vagueness of night made great distances in this dim but splendid picture, till the moon, rising over the hill-top, chased the shadows away, paled the lamps, and drew the distances together.

Touched by her light the crowd below became sonorous as a musical glass touched by the finger; the murmur of voices, the ripple of laughter, the sigh of moving silk and the flutter of a thousand fans intensified, rose blended and mixed, and dwelt in the air a nimbus of sound. The native city beyond grew more distinct, yet more unreal in the moonlight, which strengthened the black shadows of the wooded cliffs and converted the harbor into a trembling mirror.

"We shall never see anything again so beautiful as that," said Jane, "so mysterious, so strange."

He did not reply. A small hand had stolen into his; it was Campanula's. She, too, was gazing at the scene around and below them, filled with who knows what thoughts.

They were not alone here on the utmost heights; women, gayly dressed, were passing into the temple behind them to pray and clap their hands before their gods. Women surrounded them, laughing, chattering, dispelling quaint perfumes on the air from large incessantly-waving fans. From the tea houses behind the temple came the thready music of *chamècens* and sounds of unseen festivity; and from the great park beyond, through the hot night, the perfume of azaleas and the odor of the dew-wet cryptomeria trees.

"Come," said Jane, "let us go and take the picture with us before it gets dulled. I will never forget this night—there is something in the air of this place I have never felt before. No, thanks, I don't want to see the tea houses, I am quite content with this; let us go down right through it, and home."

They descended the broad flights of steps through the murmuring, laughing, and perfumed crowd. There was something in the air indeed, something as intoxicating as wine, yet far more subtle, subtle as a poison or a love philter.

They found rikshas to take them back, and the whole party returned to the hotel, where they left Jane.

"To-morrow at noon," she said to Leslie, as she turned to enter.

"Yes, or even a little later; the train doesn't start till after one."

"Good-night!" She waved her hand in the lamplit portico and vanished.

They had no need of lanterns to show the way up the hill-path to the House of the Clouds; the path was a tangle of moonlight and lilac-bough shadows, a tremulous carpet upon which above them they perceived a creeping and colored thing.

It was Cherry-blossom. She, too, had been at the festival at the O Suwa, and was now returning, wearied out and walking like a somnambulist, a lantern painted with butterflies held before her nodding at the end of a bamboo cane.

In the house, when he had fastened the shoji and taken his night lantern from Pine-breeze, he turned to where Campanula was standing, a vague figure in the dimly-lit room. Yielding to a sudden impulse he picked her up from the ground, just as he might have picked up a child, and kissed her—kissed her just as he had kissed her when she was a child that day, years ago, in the valley by the Nikko road.

That night sleep was impossible. The lights of the O Suwa burned before him, the perfume of the azaleas and cryptomerias pursued him, lighting always and leading him always to the same image—Jane.

He lay considering what the future would be when Jane was gone; the rainy season would soon be upon them, and then the autumn and the winter and the spring again after that, and the years to come.

Whilst thus torturing his soul his mind was steadfastly making a resolve. A resolve that, come what might, Jane must not go out of his life. That to-morrow he must act in such a way as to make her for ever his own.

Come what might!

There was no time left for thought, scarcely enough for action.

He had quite ceased to battle with himself, to say this is right or this is wrong. Time had cut all these arguments short with the command: "Act now, now, in the next twenty-four hours! for after that your chance is gone."

Then he began to sketch out the plan that had been vaguely forming in his brain all the evening—a plan that the villainous conduct of George du Telle made possible and practicable, and, to Leslie's mind, almost plausible.

As he lay thus, a faint sigh came through the lattice of the window. The wind had risen, and was moving the cherry branches and the azaleas.

Then came another sound—the sound of a stick tapping on the garden path, as if some blind person were cautiously feeling their way round the house.

Up along the garden path, pausing now, now advancing, now dying away, now returning, somebody was promenading in front of the house, keeping watch and ward like a sentry, somebody whose feet made no sound, somebody blind.

A feeling of sick terror came over him—terror not to be borne.

He pulled the mosquito-net aside, and rose, shivering and trembling, feeling that he must look out at all hazards—even at the worst.

He pulled the slats aside and looked out. Nobody. The moonlight lay on the azaleas and the garden path, but of the prowler there was no sign.

Then he saw the cause of the sound. A lath broken from the house wall was hanging with tip touching the path, and tapping upon it as the wind shook it.

He returned to bed, and tried to snatch a few hours' sleep, but the sound of the blind man tapping his way continued all night long—now faint, now loud, and insistent as the wind rose and fell.

CHAPTER XXVII

THE "EMPRESS OF JAPAN"

If Mr. Kamamura had sent a special messenger to Paradise to pick from the aviary there a blue-winged and bright-eyed day for his garden-party, he would not have obtained a better one than that which came by chance.

A haze hid its coming. Just after sunrise, looking from Leslie's garden one could scarcely see Nagasaki down below—a toy town, seen through faint blue gauze, it seemed. The wind came in puffs, hot from the Pacific, shaking the cherry branches.

The great double cherry-blossoms were falling. The close, even moss under the trees was white, like ground after a mild snowstorm.

There was something in the atmosphere which loosened the petals this morning. At each puff of wind a fresh shower fell, sifting through the air to scatter softly on the ground. It was a ghostly sight in the gray and silent dawn; the trees seemed despoiling themselves, casting their blossoms from them in sorrow or fear.

In the veranda stood the crimson garden umbrella, all damp with dew, and four pairs of dogs in a row. The house was deathly still; and one might have likened it to a tomb, had it not possessed so much the appearance of a bandbox, looped and latticed.

Presently a faint sound might have been heard. A panel slid back, and a figure appeared, holding in its hand a lighted paper lantern.

It was Campanula, clad in blue, her feet peeping from beneath her skirt like two white mice.

She put out the lantern, and hung it on a hook. Then she put on a pair of clogs, and clicked down the steps. She went down the path, through the little gate, and vanished from sight; and as her footsteps died away, silence returned to the house and the garden.

Then in a few minutes a glorious transformation scene took place. The haze turned to a golden mist; it became sundered by rivers of clear air, and from it leaped the sun, like Helios from the sea.

Instantly the silence of the orchard became broken by the bickering of birds; a cock crowed somewhere in the back premises, and he was answered by the cock that lived half-way down the hill at the cooper's shop—who was answered, a minute later, by all the roosters in Nagasaki.

The mist vanished entirely now, the sun began steadily to mount into the vault of perfect blue; his slanting rays shot through the cherry orchard, striking here the bole of a tree glistening with great tears of fragrant gum, and there on the ground besnowed with blossom, even the fierce old hills of the landscape garden lost something of their ruggedness in the warm and mellow light.

Then the house began to awaken. Pine-breeze appeared on the veranda, and after Pine-breeze the other Mousmès all busy, or appearing so, dragging out futon to air for a moment in the morning brightness, and lacquer screens to be dusted.

"Summer has come in the night," said Lotus-bud, pointing out the fallen cherry-blossoms.

"Yes," chimed in Pine-breeze, "but spring has gone."

"I dreamt last night of frost." This from Cherry-blossom, who was busily engaged watching the others at work.

Frost is a bad dream in Japan, and the Mousmès conferred in murmurs as to what it might mean.

"I know," said Lotus-bud suddenly, with an air of conviction.

"What?"

"The riksha man will die."

"Which?" asked Pine-breeze.

Then the two Mousmès began to "guy" Cherry-blossom as to the number of the riksha man destined to die.

"Ichi-ban, Ni-ban, San-ban,"[3] murmured Lotus-bud.

[Footnote 3: Number one, number two, number three.]

"Shi-ban, Go-ban, Roku-ban," rippled Pine-breeze.

"Hachi-ban!" suddenly cried Lotus-bud, with an air of inspiration.

"Ku-ban!" replied Pine-breeze, with the air of going one better.

"Leslie San!" said Cherry-blossom: and Pine-breeze got up and scuttered into the house, where Leslie San was calling for his bath to be heated.

An hour later he appeared on the veranda, fully dressed.

He noticed the promise of heat in the air; he noted the great fall of cherry-blossoms that had occurred during the night; he noted the lantern that Campanula had hung on the hook.

Then he left the veranda, came down into the garden path, and through the gate.

Outside the gate there was a little by-path that led upwards and to the left, between a double bank of bushes to an open space like a natural platform, from which a splendid view of the harbor and hills could be obtained, A great camellia tree forty feet high grew here, alone in its splendor, and beneath it he stood gazing at the harbor.

He could hear the faint monosyllabic cry of the brown hawks ever circling above the blue water, and the distant sound of a drum from the *Rurik* where she lay at anchor. He could see the sampans shooting hither and thither, carrying fruit and what not to the ships in the anchorage, and the Junks floating like brown phantoms past the shadow of the opposite cliffs.

But his eye was searching for something that was not there.

He looked at his watch, put it back in his pocket with an impatient gesture, and continued to gaze.

Suddenly—Hrr-'mph!—Haa-aar!—the blast of a syren came shouting up the harbor, and chasing the echoes through the hills. The brown hawks rose and circled in wild flight, and past a bend came a great, white, double-funneled steamer.

It was the Canadian Pacific boat, the *Empress of Japan*, touching at Nagasaki, and due to leave the morning following for Yokohama and Vancouver.

He watched her for a moment as she swam to her berth, beautiful and graceful as a swan. Then he turned to the house.

To-morrow morning he and Jane would be on board that boat, bound northward up the Inland Sea, past Tsu-shima, past Osaka, past Yokohama, and away across the blue Pacific to Vancouver.

The whole plan was cut and dried. Jane had given no consent; that did not matter. She would consent; he felt the power in himself to *make* her consent.

Men of his stamp, lazy, neurotic, yet strong-willed, stung into action by love or hate, sometimes assume momentary but terrible command over events; they infect with their passion, infuriate with their hate, or paralyze with their love.

He entered the house, ordered breakfast, and enquired for Campanula.

She had gone down at dawn, said Pine-breeze, to see O Toku San, the poor girl who was so ill, and was now dying. He was glad Campanula was out, and determined if possible to get his preparations over before her return. Jane and he would return from Mr. Kamamura's about six that evening. It would be time enough then to tell Campanula of his journey.

As he breakfasted, he completed that part of his plans which had reference to Campanula.

She would be safe and well looked after by M'Gourley, till—he came back. He told himself he would come back some day; perhaps in six months or so he would come back.

And why should he worry about leaving Campanula for a time? He had often gone away before, once as far as London; he had always come back.

Why should Campanula mind his going away again?

Why, indeed!

He tried to forget how her little hand had stolen into his on the evening before as if for protection. How, when he had kissed her, she had suddenly flung aside her timid reserve, and with her arms around his neck, but without a word, had told him what only a woman can tell without speech.

Perhaps it was because he loved her far more than he knew, that his mind was filled with gloom and apprehension.

But it was the time for action, not for thought; only a few hours lay before him in which to prepare for this journey—the journey from which he would return quite soon perhaps.

He would leave the house just as it was to Campanula and the Mousmès till he came back and made other arrangements. M'Gourley, as his agent, would supply them with all the money needful just as he had done before.

Then he called Pine-breeze and told her to get his portmanteau up to his room, as he was going on a journey.

He packed hurriedly, whilst Lotus-bud handed him things. He wanted to get the packing over and done with.

The strong sunlight reflected from the matting lit up the room with a golden glow. Pine-breeze in the kitchen below was singing a song about a lilac bough—the same song he had heard in the orchard that day when Campanula had cried: "Hist, some one at the gate!"

He leaned back sitting on his heels to listen. He heard the end of the song now. He did not hear it that day, for Jane, knocking at the veranda, had cut it short.

This was the gist of the last verse:

"The bee comes no moreWhen the lilac's white blossom is dead."

Then he went on with his packing at a furious rate, stuffing in shirts, collars, handkerchiefs, his mind wandering over all sorts of subjects.

His packing finished, he went to the window, took out his pocketbook, and examined its contents. Three hundred and ten pounds, half in circular notes, half in notes of the Bank of England.

Then he took out a check-book and a stylograph pen, and wrote a check for five hundred, payable to himself.

Ten minutes later he was in a riksha making for the Bund, where he stopped at Holme & Ringers, the shipping agents, bought two first-class tickets for Vancouver, and changed his check, receiving part in cash, and part in a check upon the National Specie Bank of Yokohama.

It was now eleven o'clock, and he had practically completed his preparations. He had now to see Mac, and he turned his steps to the office, which was only a stone's throw from the shipping agents. Mac was writing letters.

"Morning," said he, glancing up, and seeming surprised to see his partner at that hour.

"What's agate?"

"I am," said Leslie, trying to assume a jovial manner. "I'm off for a holiday, and I want you to look after things same as you've done before."

"This is sudden," said Mac, going on with his correspondence without looking up.

"Oh, it's never too sudden for a holiday. And see here, I'd better leave you some ready cash: here's a check for two fifty. I want you to look after the bairn whilst I'm away."

"Keep the money," said Mac, "and pay me—when y' come back. Ay, ay, it'll be soon enough then—soon enough then."

"I'd sooner leave you the money."

"Weel, put it in that drawer."

"Well, you *are* a bear this morning. See here, I've put it in the drawer, but I'll see you again before I go: I'm not off till to-morrow."

"Imphim!" replied the Dour One, and Leslie went off.

Your true Scot has a very nasty habit of expressing his bad opinion of a man. He does it in a round-about way, using hints and innuendoes, instead of coming to the matter by a direct route.

What Mac suspected or what he knew, Leslie could not tell; judging from his manner, however, he knew or suspected a lot.

However, he had no time to trouble about Mac. He had one thing more to do before meeting Jane, Mr. Initogo the landlord had to be interviewed, and the rent paid.

There was a fair of a sort on in the street that formed the shortest cut to Mr. Initogo's. It was filled with a many-colored crowd, flags were fluttering, awnings flapping in the wind; every shop had some extra advertisement to attract customers, and during the past night, like mushrooms, extra booths had sprung into being.

A roaring trade was going forward; here, all kinds of fruit, there all kinds of fish, some with bunches of violets in their mouths; cakes reposing on branches of cherry or myrtle; cakes in the form of donkeys and monkeys and goats; cakes shaped like spinning-tops; cakes in the shape of suns, moons and stars; candied beans, beans mixed with comfits, kites, masks, and paper dragons. Paper fish shaped like carp for the Little-boys' Festival of the 5th of May.

The noise and bustle somehow pleased Leslie, and soothed him; and he drifted along with the chattering stream of men, women, Mousmès, little boys and mere babies. Some of the children had long, curved trumpets of glass, from which they blew the most horrible of hobgoblin sounds. Here a man was frying pancakes, wrapping them in rice paper, and flinging them to unseen customers in the crowd, who flung him back the money. Here a person in spectacles, who looked like a professor of chemistry gone mad, was blowing from a glass-blower's tube dragons and fish in sugar-candy. Apothecaries, with great golden eyes painted on their booths, were selling little rice paper charms, one to be taken dissolved in water for the stomach-ache, two for lumbago, three for migraine. Here stood a man who would pull your teeth out with his fingers, three sen a tooth.

The cheap curio dealers were in evidence with their wares cheap and bad; those quaint perambulating curio dealers, who, as a rule, only start business at sundown, and whose stock-in-trade include old top hats, old boots, old—anything—European. "Caw—caw—caw!" You look up, and see a great kite straining at its strings.

And then the umbrellas! Leslie had a good view of them, for he was head and shoulders taller than any one in the crowd. Red, pink, gray, gray-green, pink-and-white, blossom-bestrewn, stork-bestrewn, a shifting mass of color reflecting the sunlight.

But though he saw all this, and though the noise and bustle and laughter and general atmosphere of festivity fell in with his humor, his thoughts were far away at Osaka; he was wondering what George du Telle was doing, and what George du Telle would say in a day or so, and how he would look. He had never hated George du Telle really till now that he had determined to rob him of his wife.

Now that he was about to commit, or attempt to commit, a vile and abominable act against George du Telle, that person seemed to him the acme of all things vile and abominable.

Suddenly, through an opening in the crowd, Leslie caught a glimpse of a face, the face of a blind man, stolid, stony, with a flattened nose and wearing an indescribable expression of eld, weariness, and misfortune.

It was only a momentary glimpse, but revealed just for a moment, and contrasted with the shifting colored mass around him, with the noise and laughter, the sunlight and the movement of life, it was like a vision of death.

Leslie stood for a moment startled and chilled; the joyous exaltation in his mind a moment ago had vanished: it was as if a cloud had come between him and the sun.

Why were these things always occurring to fret his soul and trouble his imagination? This blind man was nothing but an ordinary blind man of Japan such as one might see any day. The broken lath that had troubled him all night was but a broken lath; the song of the mushi that had started that infernal sound in his head was but the sound of an insect buzzing; the azalea that had caused that frightful dream was but a flower.

These slight things, he told himself, acting on a brain made over-sensitive by opium, were not warnings, but simple causes of complex effects. And he passed on his way, cursing himself for a fool, till he reached the shop of Mr. Initogo.

That gentleman, for a wonder, was not making tea, but the sight of Leslie San instantly inspired the desire for his favorite beverage, caused him to clap his hands, and the tea-tray to appear in the hands of his wife almost instantly upon the sound.

He received his rent, which he put away with an appearance of indifference, expressed sorrow on hearing that Leslie was going away for even a short time, but joy at the thought that the journey might benefit his honorable health.

He was really fond of Leslie, this old Japanese gentleman; but the worst of the flowery Japanese language is that it remains always, so to speak, at boiling point, and towards friend or perfect stranger is the same. You can't cool it, and you can't warm it.

Whilst they were talking Kiku came in; her eyes were red and she had a snuffle in her voice.

She had been, it seems, to see the poor girl who was dying, O Toku San; Campanula was with her.

"Ah, yes," said Mr. Initogo, as his daughter retired upstairs. "Most sad, poor girl. A man whom she loved left her, and she is dying of it, just as a flower dies from want of water."

Leslie looked at his watch: it was after twelve. He hastened from the shop of Mr. Initogo, and securing a riksha drove to the Nagasaki Hotel on the Bund.

CHAPTER XXVIII

M'GOURLEY'S LOVE AFFAIR

At about three o'clock on that eventful day M'Gourley met one of Holme & Ringer's clerks in the street.

"So your partner's off for a holiday," said the clerk.

"So he tells me," replied Mac.

"He's going pretty far afield," went on the clerk; "Vancouver isn't—"

"Where did you say?" cut in M'Gourley.

"Well, he's bought two tickets for Vancouver this morning, one for his cousin and one for himself. She is married, and they are going to pick her husband up at Yokohama," he went on, smiling slightly.

"Vancouver!" said Mac. He stood for a moment in astonishment, then hailing a passing riksha he jumped into it, and told the driver to take him to the House of the Clouds.

Campanula had just returned, she was in the garden; and when she heard his step coming up the hill path she came to the gate to meet him.

She greeted him with a smile, but there was something about her that struck M'Gourley strangely.

She had a far-away look in her face, and she wore an abstracted air. Away from the world her mind seemed wandering in some far, strange country, whilst her little body walked beside him, and her lips answered his questions, and told him things.

"O Toku San is dead," said she; "I have just left her." She spoke gravely, but without any sorrow in her voice; one might even have imagined that she was referring to some good fortune that had fallen on O Toku San; and perhaps, indeed, she was.

"Ay! puir thing, is she?" said Mac, whose mind was also astray.

He asked had Leslie returned, and Campanula told him that he had gone to a garden-party at Omura, and would not return till evening.

"He is going away," finished Campanula, pausing on the veranda steps and unlatching the strap of her sandal.

"Oh! so he's told you?" said Mac.

Campanula said nothing; possibly she did not hear the question, so absorbed was she by her own ideas and thoughts. Suddenly she said, turning to Mac, who was leaning his shoulder against the veranda post and feeling in his pocket for his tobacco-pouch:

"I saw the Blind One to-day as I was leaving O Toku San's. I did not speak to him; he spoke to me. He said the master of the house on the heights is going on a journey from whence he will not return. Then he went away. A wind from the hill blew my kimono apart and a chill came to my breast. I do not know who the Blind One is—perhaps he is Death."

M'Gourley, as she spoke, noticed that she had refolded her kimono from right to left instead of from left to right.

Now in Japan, the only people who wear their kimonos folded from right to left are the dead.

He felt sick and shivery at the words she had just spoken, and he could not reply to them or ask questions; he was filled with a horror of the subject, a dead, blind terror of it. He looked down and said gruffly:

"What way is that you've folded your kimono? Just run into the house and put it right. I'll bide here on the verandy and smoke my pipe."

She vanished into the house, and Mac sat down, but he did not light his pipe. What could be the meaning of all this? Surely he was dead, and laid long ago in the green woods of Nikko—could it be possible that the dead return?

Why was it that she alone could see him, hear him, and speak to him?

His eye caught the crimson azaleas as they bloomed in their beauty and splendor, and the Nikko road rose before him, the mysterious valley, peopled by the crimson flowers, the cypress trees, the far-off country, and the distant sea hills beyond Tanagura.

He heard Leslie's voice as it denied the existence of God, and declared that if he had ever been given a creature that loved him, he would have cared for and loved it.

Then he felt something touch his shoulder, and, turning with a start, found it was Campanula.

"Come," said she, in the manner of a person who would say, "I wish to show you something."

He rose and followed her into the house. She led the way upstairs, and down the narrow passage to Leslie's room.

At the door she paused and pointed to an object on the floor. It was a portmanteau packed and strapped.

They both looked at it without saying a word: a silence, that spoke of the deep, unconscious understanding between them.

"Come," said Mac in his turn, and taking her by the hand he led her downstairs.

Had the portmanteau been a coffin, containing some being beloved by Campanula, he could not have spoken more gently, or led her away from it more tenderly.

Downstairs the old, rough, gruff M'Gourley seemed very much perturbed.

Could he have found Leslie alone at that moment, a very regrettable scene might have ensued.

And yet at the bottom of all his anger and perturbation lay a golden gleam. If Leslie went off like this, Campanula would be all his (Mac's) own.

He had no idea of marrying her, or anything of that sort; but he had an immense idea of possessing her all for himself.

He had, proposed to buy a half share in her at Nikko, and he would have made a bad bargain, for during the last five years he had possessed a full half share without paying a cent, unless we count the pounds and pounds expended on dolls, sweets, and so forth.

But this was not like having her all to himself: a creature to feed and clothe, to buy hairpins for and tabis, fans and sweets; to listen to of an evening, as her fingers strayed over the strings of a *chamècen*, or her tongue told fabulous tales of folk clad in fur or feathers.

All at once, as he paced the room, he turned to her, literally picked her up, hugged her, gave her a kiss, and said: "He'll come back to you. Dinna greet; I canna stand it. I'll be back and see you the morrow morn before he goes."

He hurried out of the house, and went raging down the hill.

To be in anger with one whom one loves works, indeed, like madness in the blood.

Mac, as he plunged down the hill, was lashing himself into a fury against Leslie. He turned into a saki shop and drank half a pint of that seemingly innocuous liquor; then he went to the office, took a whisky bottle from a cupboard, and poured himself out a liberal peg.

He was an abstemious man as a rule, but once he took the bit between his teeth nothing on God's earth except death would stop him, till the next morning's headache came.

At five he recognized that he was hopelessly embarked on a grand drunk, and determined to take a riksha over to Mogi; there complete the business, and return in time next morning to see Leslie before he started.

Just before starting from the hotel a waiter brought him out a cablegram from Shanghai, which had come round from the office. It was relative to a bank disaster that had occurred in India. He read it, stuffed it into his pocket, and ordered the Djin to proceed.

CHAPTER XXIX

THE GARDEN-PARTY

Within an hour of the great city of Nagasaki, in the midst of a park that was at the same time half a garden, lay the country residence of Mr. Kamamura; once a man who carried two swords, with the longer of which he would have beheaded you for two words and have done it with neatness and despatch, now a gentleman in a frock-coat and tall hat, wearing gold-rimmed glasses and a smile.

The long, low house, white as snow and surrounded by a narrow veranda, faced west, and was surrounded by a garden recalling the gardens of Dai Nichi Do: a garden filled with the music of fountains and the poetry of birds.

Alas! on the day of his garden-party Mr. Kamamura, seized with the spirit of modernity and the savagery of civilization, not content with the music of heaven, and prompted, no doubt, by the devil, had hired a brass band and placed it in a little kiosk, with orders to bray Strauss in the face of Nature from three o'clock till dusk.

There were many guests, and the gardens soon presented an animated appearance. Many of the ladles had retained the national dress, and marvelous were the fabrics to be seen in the form of the obi or flowing loose in the graceful kimono.

Some of the guests surrounded a pair of jugglers, two terrible men dressed in red, who fenced with and transfixed one another with long swords, swallowed fire, and belched it like dragons.

In another corner of the grounds fireworks were whizzing and cracking, filling the clear air above with a thin blue haze through which, just as Jane and Leslie entered the grounds, there rose a wonderful fire balloon made of colored paper and fashioned in the form of a turkey cock.

"It's like a party in the lunatic asylum," whispered Jane, as they threaded the maze of guests in search of their host and hostess. "And, Dick, you *do* look perfectly awful in that panama amongst all these men in tall hats—I mean they look awful beside you, but they are *de rigueur*; and it's better to be *de rigueur* and look frightful, than to be not *de rigueur* and look nice. How d'y' do?" and Jane extended her arm, pump-handle fashion, to the little gentleman with the sallow face to whom Leslie was introducing her.

"Much pleasure, much pleasure," said Mr. Kamamura, whose English was mixed and limited, and who, like Kiku San, had not completely mastered the letter "l." "Will the honorable rady so make equal health Nagysaki (the proper way to pronounce Nagasaki) you stay? So good. Over there Mrs. Kamamura;

you make known;" and Mr. Kamamura presenting his arm Jane was led away through the crowd like some tall and graceful frigate threading a maze of painted cock-boats.

Leslie, left to himself, turned with a gloomy expression of countenance to where the jugglers were dislocating each other's necks. He did not see them; he was looking out of the side of his eyes at Jane.

She had been led across one of the willow-pattern bridges, and he could see her now standing at one of the kiosks, a tea-cup in her hand. She was talking to Mr. Kamamura and a little lady in European dress—Mrs. Kamamura, probably.

What could they be talking about? Conversation, probably, sufficient to dislocate the gravity of a Socrates.

He turned his head impatiently and tried to take an interest in the jugglers, without success. There was something deeply irritating about the scene of frivolity in which Fate had staged the last scenes of the most important act in his life.

The *Empress of Japan* sailed at eight on the morrow morning, and as yet he had made no movement as regards Jane. All this trifling was but a bad prelude to those words so soon to be spoken.

He little knew that Tragedy stood at his elbow in the form of James Anderson, manager to M'Cormick, the great silk dealers on the Bund.

"Why, Leslie, man! I thought I knew the nape of your neck. How are you?"

"Hullo, Anderson!" said Leslie, returning the other's hand-grip. "What are you doing here?"

"I'm just looking round," said Anderson. "I'm just looking round, and you'll admit it's worth the turning of one's head. I shouldn't mind exchanging places with Kamamura. It's not a bad life, his, by a long penny. This affair will bang a hole through a good pile of ten pun notes. They tell me those balloons made like dicky-birds cost—I forget now, but it's a good pile of dollars a-piece, for every feather is painted correct, and that's just like the Japs—make a pretty thing, and then stick it away in some hidey-hole where no one can see it, or burn it—What's agate now?"

The crowd was in motion, flooding towards a part of the grounds where a little stage had been erected, backed and half surrounded by cypress trees. On the stage, against the dark-green background, could be seen the graceful figure of a girl.

She was dancing. It was a dance that at first insipid, became after a few moments fascinating, lulling, exquisite to watch as the movements of a flower blown by the wind.

They drew close and stood to look. The girl was dressed in amber and scarlet, with a scarlet flower in the night of her hair—a *bijou rose et noir*, recalling Baudelaire's Lola de Vallence.

Her supple body seemed inspired by the mysterious music we hear wandering through the land of spring, and expressing itself in the voices of the wind and the birds and the streams.

She seemed to have learned her art in the academy where the daffodils are taught to dance and the bluebells to make their bow.

"It's the Geisha Kamamura has hired—paid her something like two hundred to dance that fan-dance, or whatever they call it. She was a Tokyo girl, and had left the business to get married, but she couldn't withstand the two hundred; the best Geisha in Japan, they say. What's this her name? O something San. Hoots! but my memory is gone fishing to-day. Listen! she's talking."

The dance had ceased, and the girl, in the silence that followed the tinkling of the three accompanying *chamècens*, had commenced one of those poetical recitals in favor with an intellectual Japanese audience.

Her recitation was sad; it bemoaned the thing we call change. The cherry-blossom is fair, ran this untranslatable poem, but it must die and give place to the lotus.

"I cannot understand this depression in trade," murmured the muted voice of Anderson, as he stood beside Leslie. "It's been spreading and spreading, and there's nothing it hasn't spread into."

And the lotus parts with its petals to give place to the chrysanthemum, the Royal chrysanthemum.

"We've had a good year till now, ourselves, but hech! man, there's a matter of fifteen thousand gone over the breaking of the Bombay and Benares bank—clean gone, never to come back—and that takes the sugar off the cake—ay, the devil himself won't whistle it home again."

And the gray winter sky and the snowflakes, like ghosts of flowers, finished the poem of the Geisha, whilst Leslie stood transfixed for a second, frozen by the news he had just heard, and unable to turn. He turned round full on Anderson.

"The breaking of *what*?"

"The Bombay and Benares. Have you not heard the news? It came by cable to-day at one o'clock. Good God! man, you hadn't much money in it, had you?"

"Everything—everything," said Leslie in a stammering voice. "I'm smashed."

He linked his arm in Anderson's, and dragged him along hurriedly. He wanted to go, nowhere in particular, but just get away from the spot where Anderson had sentenced his future to death.

"Man, I'm sorry! Man, I'm sorry!" said his companion. "I should not have told you so sudden, but how was I to know?"

"Smashed—smashed—smashed!" said the other, talking as a man talks in his sleep.

He held Anderson by the arm as he spoke. All around spread the many-colored crowd; fans were fluttering, umbrellas bobbing, tongues chattering, soft women's voices inlaid like music of gold on the silvery music of the fountains and cascades.

"Anderson, man, are you sure they've broken—sure?"

"Ay, ay, sure. Better to tell you straight. Sure as my name's James Anderson."

Boom! Boom! Boom! the band broke into a march by Gungl, and Leslie, releasing Anderson, ran after a figure in the crowd some twenty paces distant.

"Jane! I must speak to you at once."

Jane looked up from the little Japanese gentleman who was escorting her, saw the distress in her countryman's face, and dismissed Asia with a bow.

"I have just had frightful news. Come with me to some quiet place till I tell you about it. Anywhere. No matter where. See! there are no people across that bridge where the trees are; let us go there."

Jane spoke not a word, but he saw that she was very pale and trembling. That weakness of Jane's gave him a strange sensation. It said something that her lips had never uttered.

They passed over the little bridge. They passed over another bridge; there were no people here, only trees; they went no further.

They were in a small forest. The garden was lost to sight; only the music of the band, muted by distance, told of the festivity so near, yet apparently so far away.

The trunk of a felled tree lay in the path; they sat down upon it by common consent. Leslie took out his watch, and looked at it attentively. Then, still holding it open in his hand, he spoke.

"I want you to listen to me for five minutes—only five minutes; you can hold the watch, and measure the time yourself. Jane, when a man is going to be hanged, they will give him a glass of brandy to help him along to the drop. Will you do the same by me—give me five minutes' clear speech, and let me say just what I please without interruption; will you?"

"Yes," said Jane, and she shivered as she spoke the word. She had maintained a strange silence; impulsive as she was, one might have expected her to implore him to tell her the worst, and have it over. Perhaps she understood dimly that Leslie's disaster was personal to herself, a cataclysm the effect of which would reach her future as well as his.

"You remember," he said, after a moment's pause, "how I asked you to marry me long ago, and everything that happened after? Well, when I think of all that, it seems to me that I must have passed through life in a state of insanity, and only awakened to consciousness now. Jane, I am feeling now as a man must feel when he wakes in hell, and remembers—No matter, it is all done with now; and even if you loved me as well as I love you, it's all over and done with and useless now."

He leaned forward with his face in his hands. Jane did not speak; the music of the band had ceased, and the only sound to be heard was the weary sighing of the warm wind in the pine-tops.

"I'm broken utterly, I have just heard the news. Don't think I brought you here to listen to me whining about my misfortunes. I brought you here to tell you I love you. I meant to have carried you off in the steamer that sails to-morrow morning for the north-west. With the money I had yesterday, I would have supported you, I would have torn you out of society, and made you love me. I would have made you a Paradise. Yes, by the living God, a Paradise, or there's no such thing as love. But now I'm a beggar, and I love you too well to drag you into my ruin, and it's Fate, Fate, Fate that has done it all, and cursed be its name!"

Again silence, broken only by a faint, dreary sound. Jane was weeping.

"Don't, for the love of God!" cried Leslie. "Don't cry, or you'll make me cry too. Oh, miserable life! why was I ever born into it?" And he moved his hands in the air, as blind Samson might have done amidst the pillars of the temple.

A bird piped three times in the recesses of the wood, three flute-like notes sweet as the notes of a bell-bird. They were answered by its mate in the branches above.

Leslie put his hands to his ears, as if to shut out the happy sounds.

Jane's tears had ceased, but she did not speak, she did not breathe; only a deep sigh occasionally escaped from her.

"And now, we can only say good-bye. Let us part here for ever. We will meet again in—Heaven," said Leslie, with a horrible shuddering laugh.

He stretched out his hand and took hers. She let him have it without seeming to know that he had taken it.

She was murmuring his name in a whisper, staring at him and through him, and as if her gaze was fixed on some terrible catastrophe beyond.

"Dick! Dick! Dick!" All poetry could not express the helpless, hopeless sorrow she put into those three little whispered words.

Suddenly, filtering through the wood, came a sound, a voice, a spirit, that unrolled around them a panorama of loch, moor, and sky, hills purple with heather, lakes dark with shadow. "Auld Lang Syne."

The band was playing it, villainously enough, but the distance smoothed away the defects.

It broke Jane down. She leaned against his shoulder and sobbed like a child, and then, with both hands upstretched, she drew his face down to hers and murmured—no matter what.

Then all at once—heedless of ruin, forgetting all things, carried away on the dumb tide of passion, the wave that had retreated before disaster, only to come shoreward again resistless and gigantic—all at once, and without a word, he took her in his arms.

It was the eloquence of passion and despair, the speech without tongue of a soul tormented and *in extremis.*

It broke Jane down utterly. Hopeless, haggard, and pale as a person in the midst of some terrible disaster, she clung to him, whispering in his ear words repeated over and over again, with that reiteration which forms the rhetoric of the dying and the lost.

She had cast everything aside, the world, her position in society, her husband, her wealth. Passion and pity, that strange combination, had for the moment blinded her eyes to everything but the man beside her—but did she love him? Fate had not yet disclosed the answer to that old fatal question, that sphinx-like question whose answer forms the plot of each man's story.

CHAPTER XXX

THE FALSE REPORT

Mr. Kamamura never again saw his two tall English guests.

As a matter of fact, they sought for and found a means of leaving his garden by a back way that brought them to a road which in its turn brought them to the station.

And the native gentlefolk in the train, which brought them back to Nagasaki by six o'clock, could not imagine what great grief it was that made the tall English lady so pallid, and so like the very picture of woe.

At the Nagasaki station Leslie helped his companion into a riksha.

"Don't come back with me to the hotel," she murmured; "I will drive there alone. I want to be alone, quite alone for a while. All our arrangements are made, and there is nothing more to be said. God help me!—God help us both! Good-bye, Dick, for the present."

He watched her drive off. Then he took a riksha himself, and ordered the man to take him to the House of the Clouds.

Everything was arranged. Jane was to be his for ever. But there was no triumph in the thought. The battle had been won by his own weakness, not by his strength. Jane's compassion for him had betrayed her.

They were to sail to-morrow by the *Empress of Japan*. He was to stay the night at the hotel, for he could not possibly remain the night at the House of the Clouds having once bidden good-bye to Campanula.

Beyond Vancouver lay the scheme traced out by him, accepted by Jane. They were to buy a farm in the Canadian North-west, and live there for ever happily. He would not touch a penny of her money; he had jewelry worth at least four hundred pounds, which would be amply sufficient to start on. His share in M'Gourley's business was to be left for Campanula.

It is true he knew little about farming, but—love can do anything.

Viewed from a natural standpoint the whole arrangement was not only natural but praiseworthy. That a woman, fond of a natural life in the open air, should leave a creature like George du Telle, and cast herself into the arms of a man like Leslie. What could be more in keeping with the grand aim of Nature, the propagation of the fit in body?

Viewed from a social standpoint the whole arrangement was wickedly absurd. And from a moral standpoint simply wicked.

Nature stood decidedly on Leslie's side; God (according to the theologians) and society stood against him.

These problems are occurring every day and every minute of the day, perplexing the thinker and confounding his belief, unless he looks upon the world as a higher thing than a breeding ground for animals. And it is generally by their side issues they are to be solved, and the side issue in Leslie's case was Campanula.

He was nearing Danjuro's shop when he saw a riksha with a disguised figure in it.

It was Mac, and Mac was disguised with whisky.

He was flushed, and his hat was on the back of his head, and he was so obviously fuddled that the gentle Japanese who passed smiled and passed on, without looking back.

"Stop!" cried Leslie to his man, then jumping out he ran to M'Gourley's riksha, which had also stopped.

"Have you heard the news?"

"News?" said Mac. "News—what news?"

"The Bombay and Benares bank is broken."

"It is not," replied the other, fumbling in his pocket. "Na, na—false report. Bombay and Ta-Lien, you mean." Then, drawing a paper from his pocket, and with ferocity: "Canna ye read?"

Leslie took the paper; it was a cablegram from Shanghai.

> "False report. Bombay and Ta-Lien suspended. Bombay and Benares safe.
>
> JARDINE MATHESON."

"Good Heavens!" said Leslie. "When did you get this?"
"Hoor ago. Drive on, you—wheel me awa'."
"Where are you going?"
"Mogi—to forget I was ever such a fule as to go into partnership with a man like—*wheel me awa'!*"
"Steady on, steady on," said Leslie.
"I'll be back the morrow morn and see y' before you're awa' to Vancouver."
Then, leaning back as the riksha started: "I may be a fule, but I'm not a blind fule, and I'm not a—(*hic!*)."
The riksha joggled over a stone and he collapsed like a shut-down opera hat. Leslie continued his way.

CHAPTER XXXI

FAREWELL

It was seven o'clock; the birds were taking their nests in the cherry orchard with one final burst of chattering. The sky in the west, wave-green melting into vaguest blue, held one solitary cloud floating like a rose-leaf beneath the evening star. Leslie stood at his gate, looking for the last time at the twilight stealing over Nagasaki. He had just arrived.

M'Gourley's words were still ringing in his ears, and his mind was in a turmoil.

He was in exactly the position of the man who has cheated unwittingly at cards, who has found out his mistake, and who has still time to save his honor.

If the Bombay and Benares bank was safe, it was his plain duty to go at once to Jane du Telle and inform her of the fact. She was laboring under the impression that he was a ruined man. Half of her sympathy, the whole of the present situation, had arisen from that misconception. To leave her under this delusion would amount to fraud—the meanest of all frauds.

He was feeling this keenly, but unfortunately his mind, instead of grappling with the situation, and forcing his body to act, was engaged in cursing Fate, and the tangled net in which he found himself taken.

Was it his fault that the false news had come just at the psychological moment, the news that had actually thrown Jane into his arms? He kept asking himself this, as he gazed across the dusk-eyed harbor to the hills now becoming dimmed by the twilight.

This last touch of Fate would, if he accepted it without resistance, rob him of the last remnants of honor and all self-respect.

His hand was upon the stakes, he had a moment to decide whether to take them or leave them: to be a thief or an honest man.

Suddenly, as if silence had placed her finger upon their throats, the birds in the orchard ceased their chatter.

The warm day dying seemed to have called all the spirits of beauty from air and earth and sea, to stain the skies above its death-bed with the tints of the ocean and the dawn. Over the tomb of light Color, Light's firstborn child hovered like some exquisite ephemera whose wings change from beauty to beauty before dissolving for ever in darkness and death.

The silence that had come over the orchard was broken occasionally by little outbursts of squabbling from over-full nests, sounds like the flirting of a fan amongst the leaves, chirrupings that told of differences made up. Then final and complete silence that would last till night woke the owls.

Leslie at the gate suddenly made a gesture as if he were flinging something away, turned on his heel, and came towards the house.

He entered just as Cherry-blossom, with a white flower in her hair, her amber sleeves fallen back and exposing her fore-arms, her body stretched to its fullest height on the tips of her tabis, was in the act of lighting the big hall-lamp. She looked like a little cat stretching herself.

A pang went through his heart. He would never see Cherry-blossom light the big hall-lamp again, never again see Pine-breeze bring in the tea-cups, nor Lotus-bud carrying off Sweetbriar San to his box in the kitchen.

You cannot possibly live in Japan without loving your maid-servants. I mean by love that sort of passion which was inspired in Matthew Prior by the lady of fashion aged five.

It was a feature of the House of the Clouds that sometimes on the lower floor you would find a hall with two rooms on either side of it, and sometimes two rooms and no hall, and sometimes, in very hot weather, one huge room. The sliding paper partitions made this possible; nay, very easy, for Mr. Initogo had improved upon the ordinary Japanese method, being of an inventive turn of mind.

He looked into the room on the right of the hall. A *chamècen* lay on the floor, an hibachi showed a crimson spark, and a dwarf maple in a pot of Arita ware displayed its pretty form vaguely in the twilight.

He looked into the room on the left: no one.

Where was Campanula? She must have returned by this, surely. Perhaps she was upstairs.

He went up, making little noise in his stocking-feet. At the door of his room he peeped in.

There was Campanula. Oh, desolate sight! She was sitting on his big portmanteau all alone in the dusk. Her head was bent.

She looked so forlorn and so small, and the sash of her obi so huge in comparison with the wearer, that he could not but recall how she sat that morning in the Tea House of the Tortoise. That morning, when she had likened herself to a lump of mud; the morning he had proposed to adopt her, and care for her, and make her a chattel of his own.

A moment later, he had caught her up in his arms. She did not resist, but he seemed to have taken up a lifeless thing.

As he carried her downstairs, had he known, it might have seemed strange to him that so great a grief should be so light a burden.

He brought her to the room on the right, where Cherry-blossom had just lit the lamp, and sat down beside her on the matting.

He took a cigarette from his pocket, and approached the tobacco-mono with it. Then, without lighting it, he flung the cigarette away.

"Campanula, I am going on a journey. I did not tell you last night, for I had not made up my mind."

"I have heard it," she replied. She sat there beside him, a small figure with head bowed and hands folded in her lap; and the sadness and sorrowful sweetness of those four words pierced his heart.

To get this terrible interview over, to tear himself away at once, he would have sold years of his life. But it had to be gone through with.

Whether she loved him as a woman loves a man, or a child loves a father, she loved him, loved him as no person had ever loved him before—and he knew it.

Then he talked to her, telling her that he would come back.

"I have been away before, Campanula, and I have returned. Will you not believe me that I will return?"

"Ah yes," she answered, "but you did not go with her."

He said nothing for a moment. There was a sound outside; it was the coolie he had ordered to take his portmanteau to the hotel. He heard Pine-breeze accosting him, he heard him go upstairs and come down again, walking heavily. It was like the sound of a man carrying out a coffin.

He heard his steps on the garden walk dying towards the gate.

How had she discovered with whom he was going?

If she would only weep or cry out, or move, or break in some way this terrible stillness. If she would only reproach him. But she said nothing, nor even sighed. She seemed like a person stricken not by grief, but death. Then he began to talk again, telling her of the arrangements he had made. How M'Gourley San would look after her, just as he had done before, till he came back. And he would write every week—till he came back. And they would all be happy together again, as happy as ever they had been—when he came back.

To which she replied:

"If you are going away to find happiness, my happiness is great."

Fancy a white house, lantern-lit, and steeped in dusk, a tall man walking away from it rapidly, three Mousmès on their knees on the veranda crying after the vanishing form: "Come again, oh, condescend to come again quickly!"

The sound of their voices rings in his ears as he passes through the little gate. He hears it pursuing him like the faint murmur of bees, until a puff of wind blows it away and replaces it by the faint sound of the city below.

Come again! He will never come again to lie in the hammock beneath the cherry trees. Never more shall Lotus-bud hand him the night lantern to light him to his bed, nor thy small hands, O Pine-breeze, bear him the brown leather cigar-case that thy small nose loved to smell!

As he came down hill towards Nagasaki he felt as though he were leaving spring for ever behind him.

Thrice he stopped as if to return, and stood gazing into the darkness of the uphill path, listening to the wind in the branches of the lilac trees.

The last of these pauses ended more abruptly than the others, and he plunged on again down hill through the gloom.

CHAPTER XXXII

HER HOUSE IN ORDER

Left alone, Campanula sat, her hands folded in her lap—a Lost One indeed.

Before her mental vision, beyond Japan, beyond that desolate country always surrounded with ice, the country where the bluebells grew—beyond all this lay the land where O Toku San had gone that day, the land where one never regrets, one never forgets, one never remembers.

He had gone to find happiness. Not one word had she spoken to hold him back or keep him by her, this true daughter of Dai Nippon, soul sister of O Gozen San, daughter in spirit of the immortal Hirose.

Cleopatra with the asp and all the mouthing heroines of history would seem cheap indeed beside this small and faithful figure to whom death was nothing, passion and personal happiness nothing beside the happiness of the being she loved.

She sat for an hour scarce moving; then she rose up. She had no more time for personal thoughts; all things had to be left in order, and her trust to the least detail faithfully fulfilled.

She called the Mousmès to her, and told them that now Leslie San had left, they would be discharged until he came back. They could go that evening to their homes in the city below. She would pay them their wages and a month in advance, and a little present for each out of money of her own. And the three kow-towed, delighted at the prospect of change and the month's money for doing nothing, and the little present besides. They never thought to ask her what she would do herself in the house alone, their butterfly brains were so filled with the thoughts of pleasure.

Then she made Lotus-bud bring all the bills owing, bills yard long and extraordinarily minute in detail. These she discharged. There were chits out, but these were Leslie's affair, and he had no doubt settled them.

She thought of Sweetbriar San the cat, and as he was fondest of Pine-breeze, she gave Pine-breeze a small sum to take him home and keep him, applying to M'Gourley San if more money were needful.

Then she went upstairs to her own room and folded neatly the obis and kimonos in the drawers of the great lacquer cabinet. In one of these drawers were things she had only, as it were, dropped from her hand; the toys she had played with as a child. Here was the doll bought in Nikko, and bouncing balls, ever so many; and in a piece of rice paper, still ferocious, but terribly old and warped, the famous dragon.

She took him out and tried to remove the paper from his sugar-candy sides, but it was stuck too tight. She put him back, and, holding the drawer with both hands, pressed her forehead against them.

As she stood like this, mute and utterly motionless, the night breeze came through the window, bearing the perfume of the azaleas.

It was as if they were calling to her, and she closed the drawer gently and turned, as if to say, "I hear."

Then she came down and found the three Mousmès waiting, each with a lighted lamp on the end of a stick, and her frail belongings on her back, luggage consisting of cardboard boxes, except in the case of Pine-breeze, who was also burdened with a basket containing Sweetbriar San.

They had received their wages, and there was nothing left for them now to do but go; which they did, after profound salaams, murmurs and declarations of personal unworthiness.

Then Campanula found herself standing alone. The only living thing beside herself in the house was the mushi, that musician of the night, already saluting its mistress with a thin stream of song. She went to the doorway where it hung, and unhooked the little cage.

CHAPTER XXXIII

THE "LA FRANCE"

The fair that had been going on all day in the street leading to the Bund was still in full swing. A lurid sight the street presented, lit by lanterns of all colors, and flare lamps near the booths.

Leslie was glad of the noise and bustle around him; one cannot think much when pressing one's way through a Japanese fair, colored lamps dancing, Mousmès laughing, and showmen shouting, rikshas passing at a trot, or attempting so to do, children blowing trumpets, babies whirling rattles, men-of-war's men from the ships in harbor walking four abreast and arm in arm, singing "Jean Francis de Nantes," or "We won't go Home till Morning." *Chamècens* and moon fiddles buzzing and tinkling, dogs barking, and gakunin wailing.

It was ten when he reached the hotel. In the entrance-hall, where the orange trees in tubs reflected the lamp-light from their glossy leaves, a Chinese hall porter in a blue silk blouse sat on guard. From the half-open door of the *salle à manger*, where a party of Russian officers were at dinner, came the sound of laughter and the clinking of glasses.

As he entered the hotel the whole world around him changed. Campanula vanished from his mind. He was no longer in Japan. He was in the same house with Jane, and in a few more hours she would be his.

The Chinaman rose from his seat when he saw Leslie enter and led him down a corridor to the door of the private sitting-room where he had dined with Du Telles. He had promised Jane to wait for her there till the morning.

The sphinx-like Celestial closed the door, and Leslie found himself alone.

The windows were open on account of the warmth, and they gave a view of the narrow mysterious harbor that seems to have been cut in the old heroic days by some giant who was also a poet. The high cliffs cast their shadows like sable robes upon the water, jeweled with the lights of the shipping. The sky all silence and stars, paling now in the moonlight, was almost the sky of Europe. Orion was there, and the Pleiades, and Cassiopæa dreaming in her diamond-studded chair.

The room itself was a strange mixture of Japan and Europe. The floor was the matted floor of Japan, the cane sofas might have been bought at Shoolbred's. The walls were as plain and unadorned as the walls of a Japanese house are wont to be—that is to say, under the fans which the hotel proprietor had fastened to them—fans from Kioto, Tokyo, and Nara crucified against the white paneling and looking like great butterflies in some giant's collection.

He lit a pipe. Jane was upstairs in some room, but there were still nine hours of waiting to be done; and he had promised that he would not go upstairs if permitted to pass the night in the hotel, but wait patiently for her to come to him at the hour of starting.

He felt that if he thought about her he would break his oath, so he drove her from his mind.

He watched the twinkling lights in the harbor; those darting about like fire-flies were the sampans; that long hulk all crusted with light was the *La France*, the ship in which Jane had intended to sail for Osaka. It was after ten now, and she was overdue to leave. That sister-hulk, equally gemmed, was the Nord Deutscher Lloyd boat leaving at dawn for Colombo. Those three lights in a triangle were the anchor lights of the great Russian cruiser *Rurik*—the ill-fated *Rurik*.

Suddenly a horn of light shot out from the bow of the *La France*, and she began to move like a glittering town towards the sea, and the wind from the west brought the faint music of a band. The *La France* had unbuoyed and was away.

He watched her as she picked her course through the shipping stealthily like a robber. Now with all side lights showing, now with them half extinguished as she veered to avoid the bell-buoy of the Atraska shoal; now a vague phantom swallowed by the shadows of the night.

The hotel was silent now, the Russians had gone off to their ship. Somewhere outside, somewhere in the gloom of the mysterious night, a *chamècen* was tinkling to the muttering of a little drum. What dancing girl was setting her steps to that tune—and where?

He rose to his feet and began to pace the room, then he turned the lamp up till it smoked, and turned it down till it was nearly out, and cursed the burner for his own stupidity.

Still the distant *chamècen* kept up its buzzing to the devil's tattoo of the distant drum.

He walked to the window and shut it. Result—absolute silence and stifling heat. No matter; anything was better than that infernal drum.

He had shut out the drum, but he had shut in a mosquito. It was in the lace curtain, and its twang brought him again to his feet. He tried to find it in the curtain, failed, pulled the whole curtain down from its attachment, and trampled it under-foot.

Silence, this time unbroken, until one of the fans upon the wall rustled, and from beneath it crept a frightful-looking spider as brown and as broad as a penny.

He did not see it; he was sitting in the arm-chair with his head between his hands, breaking his promise to Jane.

When it was broken he got up, crossed the room, opened the door, and went into the hall.

The Chinese night-porter was sitting like a figure of stone in a blouse of blue silk. Leslie went up to him, spoke some words in a low tone, and handed him some money.

The Chinaman rose and led the way upstairs. Down a passage they went till the guide stopped, pointed to a door, turned, and vanished as silently as he had come.

Leslie went to the door and knocked softly. No answer. He turned the handle, the door opened and he entered—an empty room.

A lamp was burning on a table in one corner, a bed stood close to the window: the bed was empty.

It was Jane's room, for there lay her trunks. A glove lay on the floor. He picked it up, looked at it, smelt it, and then threw it down. The dressing-table held none of those articles of the toilet one might have expected to see. Beside the lamp on the side-table lay a letter.

He had seen the letter almost on the first moment of his entering the room, with that vague, half-terrified comprehension which we may imagine in the brain of the bull when the sun-light flashes on the sword of the matadore.

He approached it now, and read the superscription: "Richard Leslie, Esq. Important."

He opened it, and a number of bank notes came out. These he laid on one side, took the letter that was with them, and began to read.

He read the letter, not as if he were reading a letter, but the face of some scoundrel he had dragged by the ears into the zone of lamplight. He envisaged it, took whole sentences in *en bloc*. He read first at the end, then in the middle, then at the beginning.

"And now good-bye for ever. Oh, Dick, don't think badly of me for this; I have only done what was right.

"When you get this I shall be gone. I am leaving by the *La France* to meet George.

"I leave you money. Half what I have is yours; remember we are cousins, and ought to help one another.

"Oh, Dick! Dick! I *can't* do what you want. I am not thinking of myself but of my people. Imagine the disgrace and ruin it would bring them. My dear old father, it would kill him."

CHAPTER XXXIV

AMIDST THE AZALEAS

It was very late at night; clouds from the Pacific were rolling over Nagasaki, and it was evident that the hot weather of the last two days had been the prelude of a storm.

The House of the Clouds, lamp-lit and deserted, cast from the opening in the shoji a long parallelogram of light that cut the darkness like a sword; a sword of light lying upon the veranda, the graveled walk, and the landscape garden.

With the darkness outside had come a great silence broken only by the wind.

Had you been standing on the veranda you would have sworn that some blind person was prowling before the house, soundless of foot and cautiously feeling his way by tapping on the ground with a stick.

It was only the lath shaken by the wind, the tireless lath that all day and all the night before had kept the echoes of the garden answering its summons, and still kept up the unwearied sound-semblance of a blind man who walked without footstep, a patient sentinel, now advancing, now retreating, now at the garden gate, now near the azaleas, and ever waiting.

The garden gate clicked, and hurried footsteps came up the path.

It was Leslie, hatless, bright and wild of eye, walking rapidly, but in a tottering manner. His lips were of a dull purple color, and he had the aspect of a man heavily drugged with opium.

He crossed the veranda and entered the deserted hall. He looked into the rooms on either side—they were both empty. Then he came back to the hall, and cried out, "Campanula!" The rafters returned the sound of his voice, but she did not answer.

He was perfectly clear of mind, but his breathing was affected, and a deadly torpor hung over him which his will alone prevented falling.

He took in all the details around him with extraordinary clearness, amongst others the fact that the mushi's cage had been removed.

Having waited for a moment, straining his ears to catch the faintest sound, he seized the swinging paper lantern that lit the hall, and with it in his hand went into the kitchen. It was deserted. Then he went upstairs—every room was empty. It was like a house from which the people had fled in terror, and he came down again, wild with the apprehension of some unknown tragedy.

He brought the lamp into the room on the right of the passage, and placed it on the floor. Something crimson lay on the primrose-colored matting. He picked it up; it was Campanula's obi. Why had she cast it there?

He was looking round him as if for a person to explain all these things, when his eye caught an open drawer of the great lacquer cabinet that contained his papers. He looked into the drawer, and it was empty. It was the drawer in which he had placed the waki-zashi—the suicide sword, given to him by Jane.

From the open drawer his eyes turned to the obi, which he had dropped, and then he looked round him, as Dives looks round him in that picture of Teniers, where Dives wakes in Hell.

As he stood, the wind shook the broken lath outside, and played with it. "Tap! tap! tap!"

He saw the sunlit Nikko road, the valley of the crimson azaleas, the Lost One who had loved him as no other being had loved him—the one he had lost for ever.

She was dead, yet it was denied to him to find her, and clasp her in his arms, and die with her.

Death was nothing, but never to find her again, never to see her again, or touch her small body, that was an agony far beyond death.

He left the room, feeling by the walls like a man without sight.

Outside, the world was in utter darkness. More clouds had rolled up over the sky, as if called by the Blind One, the tapping of whose stick betrayed him, as he walked, waiting for his prey.

If he could find her, what cared he for the Blind One! If he could not find her he felt that he would be for ever lost. But he could never find her more, for the opium sleep was falling upon him now. He had no more strength to fight it, and the darkness of the pit lay around him.

Suddenly, the night wind changed, and brought him the perfume of the unseen azaleas, and with the perfume a thin thread of song.

It was the song of the mushi—the atom of life he had spared that day in his fury, even as God might now be sparing him—the mushi she had loved so well. Feeling by the veranda wall, he followed the song like a man led by a thread, and as he came he crushed something beneath his foot: it was the lath, whose sound would never trouble him again.

He felt the azalea bushes around his knees, and advanced amongst them, still led by the tremulous song, till his foot touched something soft, and his hand a tiny cage, hanging to one of the crimson-flowering boughs.

CHAPTER XXXV

BON MATSURI

It was the 18th of August—the last night of Bon Matsuri.

Under a sky splendid with stars, the hills about Nagasaki were gemmed with colored lights. Ten thousand colored lanterns adorned the terraced cemeteries, and towards dawn each lantern would be fixed to a tiny boat of straw, freighted with a few small coins, and some small offering of fruit, to stay the souls of the dead on their long journey home.

M'Gourley had come out to see the fairy-like spectacle, for he knew that Mr. Initogo, that faithful old Pagan gentleman, was amidst the rejoicers on the hillsides, and had lit two lanterns, and freighted two small boats, for the souls of two friends he had known on earth.

Just as the morning breeze began to blow, and before the first star had paled in the dawn breaking over the Pacific, the gazers from the ships and the shore drew their breath, for suddenly the whole hillsides seemed in motion, shifting and glittering down to the water's edge, till the ripples became surrounded by a zone of rose-colored fire.

Then the water itself became dyed with the glow of ten thousand lanterns, each bravely upborne on its little ship of straw, whose sails took the Eastern breeze.

As the fairy flotilla sailed away, spreading the harbor with light and color, ship after ship took fire, and ship after ship was lost.

M'Gourley, hat in hand, stood watching till the last spark had vanished in the lilac of the dawn; then, with a sigh that spoke of things that were not, but might have been, he turned slowly home.

CPSIA information can be obtained
at www.ICGtesting.com
Printed in the USA
LVHW042212040522
717863LV00006B/397